Contents

BABY SHOWER SUGAR COOKIES

Serving: about 5 dozen. **- Prep:** 20m **- Ready in:** 30m

INGREDIENTS

- 1 cup butter, softened
- 1-1/2 cups sugar
- 1 egg
- 1 tsp. vanilla extract
- 1/2 tsp. almond extract
- 2-1/2 cups all-purpose flour
- 1 tsp. baking soda
- 1 tsp. cream of tartar

- Pink and blue colored sugar

DIRECTION

1. Cream together sugar and butter in a large bowl. Stir in egg until well combined. Add extracts and beat well. Mix cream of tartar, baking soda, and flour together; slowly beat into the creamed mixture. Chill dough for 2 hours, covered, until it's able to handle easily.

2. Roll dough out to 1/8-inch thick on a work surface lightly coated with flour. Cut dough into small feet and hands or your favorite shapes. Arrange ongreased baking sheets. Scatter top with colored sugar. Bake cookies at 375° until edges turn brown lightly, for 6 to 8 minutes. Transfer cookies to wire racks and allow to cool.

Nutrition Information

Calories: 134 calories Total Carbohydrate: 18g Cholesterol: 23 mg Total Fat: 6g Fiber: 0g Proteinr: 1g Sodium: 106 mg

BEACH BLANKET SUGAR COOKIES

Serving: 1 dozen. **- Prep:** 30m **- Ready in:** 40m

INGREDIENTS

- 1/2 cup butter, softened
- 2/3 cup sugar
- 1 large egg
- 1-3/4 cups all-purpose flour
- 1 tsp. baking powder
- 1/4 tsp. pumpkin pie spice
- 1 can (16 oz.) vanilla frosting
- Gel or liquid food coloring

DIRECTION

1. Beat sugar and butter in a large mixing bowl until fluffy and light. Add egg and beat well. Mix pumpkin pie spice, baking powder, and flour; slowly mix into creamed mixture. Chill dough, covered, for 1 hour or until easy to work with.

2. Cut dough in half. Flatten each piece of dough into a 15x8-inch rectangle on a work surface lightly dusted with flour. Cut the rectangle in half vertically; cut crosswise into thirds, collecting 6 strips. Arrange strips 1 inch apart on ungreased baking sheets. Slightly bend to shape curves in cookies, if

desired.

3. Bake cookies for 10 to 13 minutes at 350° until edges turn brown lightly. Transfer to wire racks and allow to cool. Tint frosting using food coloring; frost cookies as desired.

Nutrition Information

Calories: false Total Carbohydrate: 25g Cholesterol: 19 mg Total Fat: 7g Fiber: traceg Proteinr: 1g Sodium: 97 mg

BUTTERY SUGAR COOKIES

Serving: Makes about 4 dozen cookies - **Prep:** 1h

INGREDIENTS

- 2 sticks (1 cup) unsalted butter, softened
- 1 cup sugar
- 1/2 tsp. salt
- 1 large egg
- 1 tsp. pure vanilla extract
- 2 cups all-purpose flour
- 1 cup coarse sanding sugar (see Cooks' Note)
- Wax paper; 2 large baking sheets; parchment paper

DIRECTION

1. To make dough: In a big bowl, with an electric mixer, whisk together salt, sugar, and butter on medium-high speed, about 6 minutes with a handheld mixture or 3 minutes with a stand mixer(better to be fitted with paddle attachment), until fluffy and pale. Whisk in vanilla and egg. Decrease to low speed and blend in flour.
2. Cut dough in half; shape each half into a disk; use wax paper to wrap it. Keep each disk in one resealable plastic bag; allow to chill for 1 hour until it is firm enough to form into balls.
3. Set rack in the middle of the oven and heat oven to 350 degrees F. Line parchment paper on baking sheets.
4. To bake cookies and decorate them: During heating the oven, take out 1 piece of dough (keep the rest of dough chilled). Form one level tbsp. of dough into one ball; roll the dough ball in coarse sugar placed in a shallow bowl so it is entirely coat. (Quickly chill dough in the fridge or the freezer if it is too soft for forming the ball.)
5. Arrange ball on the lined baking tray, 2 inches apart from each other. Use the flat bottom of a glass to

flatten balls into 2-in. rounds.

6. Bake one tray of cookie at a time, about 12-15 minutes in total, till the bottoms are golden. Let cookies cool on trays for 2 minutes. Use a metal spatula to move them to racks to cool entirely. Use the rest of dough on the cooled baking trays to make additional cookies.

7. Note: There are various colors of sanding sugars and they are sold at specialty foods stores. You can use only one color or combine some colors together.

CRISP SUGAR COOKIE MIX

Serving: about 4 dozen per batch. **- Prep:** 20m **- Ready in:** 30m

INGREDIENTS

- 5 cups all-purpose flour
- 3 cups confectioners' sugar
- 2 tsps. baking soda
- 2 tsps. cream of tarta
- 1 cup butter, softened
- 1 egg
- 1 tsp. vanilla extract
- 1/2 tsp. almond extract
- Colored sugar, optional

DIRECTION

1. Mix the initial 4 ingredients in a big bowl; combine thoroughly. Keep in a dry, cool place in one airtight container for maximum of 6 months. Makes 2 batches or a total of 8 cups.

2. Prepping the cookies: cream butter in a big bowl. Whip in extracts and egg. Slowly put 4 cups of cookie mix; combine thoroughly. Refrigerate with cover for 2 to 3 hours and up to overnight.

3. Heat the oven to 375°. Unroll dough on a slightly floured counter into the thickness of 1/8-inch. Use a cookie cutter, 2-1/2-inches diameter, dipped in flour to cut the dough. Put on not greased baking sheets, an inch away. Dust using colored sugar if wished. Bake till edges turn pale browned, for 7 to 9 minutes. Transfer on wire racks to cool.

Nutrition Information

Calories: 74 calories Total Carbohydrate: 9g Cholesterol: 15 mg Total Fat: 4g Fiber: 0g Proteinr: 1g Sodium: 66 mg

CRISPY SUGAR COOKIES

Serving: about 4 dozen. **- Prep:** 20m **- Ready in:** 30m

INGREDIENTS

- 3/4 cup shortening
- 1 cup sugar
- 2 eggs
- 1/2 tsp. lemon extract
- 2-1/2 cups all-purpose flour
- 1 tsp. baking powder
- 1 tsp. salt
- Colored sugar

DIRECTION

1. Cream sugar and shortening in a big bowl till fluffy and light. Whip in extract and eggs. Mix baking powder, salt and flour; slowly put into the creamed mixture and combine thoroughly. Chill with cover for not less than 2 hours or till handleable.
2. Form dough on a floured counter into thickness of 1/8-inch. Use cookie cutters of 2-1/2-inches to cut the dough. Arrange on oiled baking sheets. Dust using colored sugar.
3. Bake about 7 to 9 minutes at 400° or till pale browned. Transfer onto wire racks to let cool.

Nutrition Information

Calories: 141 calorie s Total Carbohydrate: 18g Cholesterol: 18 mg Total Fat: 7g Fiber: 0g Proteinr: 2g Sodium: 121 mg

EASTER EGG SUGAR COOKIES

Serving: about 4-1/2 dozen. **- Prep:** 30m **- Ready in:** 40m

INGREDIENTS

- 1 cup butter, softened
- 1-1/4 cups sugar
- 3 eggs
- 1 tsp. vanilla extract

- 1/2 tsp. almond extract
- 3-1/2 cups all-purpose flour
- 1 tsp. baking powder
- 1/2 tsp. salt

Icing:

- 2 cups confectioners' sugar
- 1 tbsp. meringue powder
- 1/4 cup warm water
- 1/2 tsp. almond extract
- Liquid food coloring
- Pastel organdy ribbon (1/4 inch wide), cut into 12-inch lengths, optional

DIRECTION

1. Cream sugar and butter in a big bowl, till fluffy and light. Put in the eggs, one by one, whipping thoroughly after every increment. Whip extracts in. Mix baking powder, salt and flour; slowly put into creamed mixture. Chill with cover for an hour or till handleable.

2. Heat an oven to 375°. Unroll dough on a slightly floured counter into thickness of 1/4-inch. Cut using a 2-1/2-inch, egg-shaped, floured cookie cutter. Arrange on slightly oiled baking sheets, an-inch away. Push a plastic straw half-inch from each cookie top to create a hole for ribbon if wished.

3. Bake till pale brown for 8 to 10 minutes. Transfer onto wire racks and let cool.

4. For frosting, sift meringue powder and confectioners' sugar into one big bowl. Put the extract and water; whip at low speed to blend. Whip 5 minutes on high.

5. Put a cup of icing into a plastic or pastry bag; snip off one tiny hole from the bag corner. Use the icing to outline every cookie. Tint the rest of icing using food coloring if wished. Put in water, several drops at one time, till thin mixture, enough to smoothly flow. Fill in the middle portion of every cookie, let icing scatter to outline. Dry overnight.

6. Jazz up with the rest of the icing. Keep in airtight containers. Thread the ribbon through holes, bind ends in bow and suspend on Easter tree if wished.

Nutrition Information

Calories: 199 calories Total Carbohydrate: 31g Cholesterol: 42 mg Total Fat: 7g Fiber: 0g Proteinr: 3g Sodium: 138 mg

FOR-MY-LOVE SUGAR COOKIES

Serving: about 5-1/2 dozen. - **Prep:** 20m - **Ready in:** 30m

INGREDIENTS

- 3/4 cup shortening
- 1-1/2 cups sugar
- 2 eggs
- 3 cups self-rising flour
- 1 tsp. orange extract
- Colored sugar, optiona 1

DIRECTION

1. Cream sugar and shortening till fluffy and light in big bowl; beat extract and eggs in. Add flour slowly; stir well. Cover; refrigerate till easy to handle, 1 hour.
2. Roll dough out to 1/4-in. thick on floured surface; use lightly floured 2-in. cookie cutters to cut. If desired, sprinkle colored sugar over.
3. Put on ungreased baking sheets, 1-in. apart. Bake for 6-8 minutes till lightly browned at 375°; transfer to wire racks then cool.

Nutrition Information

Calories: 117 calories Total Carbohydrate: 17g Cholesterol: 13 mg Total Fat: 5g Fiber: 0g Proteinr: 1g
Sodium: 135 mg

GRANDMA'S FAVORITE SUGAR COOKIES

Serving: about 2 dozen. **- Prep:** 25m **- Ready in:** 35m

INGREDIENTS

- 1/2 cup butter, softened
- 1 cup plus 2 tsps. sugar, divided
- 1 egg
- 1 tsp. vanilla extract
- 2-2/3 cups all-purpose flour
- 1 tsp. baking powder
- 1/2 tsp. baking soda
- 1/2 tsp. salt
- 1/4 tsp.ground nutmeg
- 1/2 cup sour cream

- 27 to 30 raisins

DIRECTION

1. Cream together 1 cup of sugar and butter in a large bowl until fluffy and light. Whip in vanilla and egg. Mix together nutmeg, salt, baking soda, baking powder and flour. Put dry mixture into creamed mixture alternating with sour cream; beat well after every increment. Put into the refrigerator with cover until easy to handle or for 1-2 hours.
2. Roll out dough on a lightly floured surface so that it is 1/4-inch thick. Use 2-1/2-inch round cookie cutter to cut with. On lightlygreased baking sheets, arrange dough 2 inches apart from each other. Use the remaining sugar to sprinkle over. In the center of each cookie, add a raisin.
3. Put into the oven to bake at 375 degrees until the bottoms are light brown and set or for 10-12 minutes. Let it cool for 1 minute then transfer to wire racks.

HARVEST SUGAR COOKIES

Serving: 6-7 dozen (2-1/2-inch cookies). - **Prep:** 15m - **Ready in:** 25m

INGREDIENTS

- 3/4 cup butter, softened
- 1 cup sugar
- 2 eggs
- 1 tsp. vanilla extract
- 2-3/4 cups all-purpose flour
- 1 tsp. baking powder
- 1/2 tsp. salt
- Frosting of your choice or additional sugar, optional

DIRECTION

1. Cream sugar and butter in a large bowl until fluffy and light. Whip in vanilla and eggs. Mix together salt, baking powder and flour; put to creamed mixture slowly. Let it chill until firm or for 1 hour.
2. Roll the dough out on a lightly floured surface so that it is 1/4-inch thick. Use a lightly floured leaf or pumpkin cookie cutter or others to your liking to cut dough with. On agreased baking sheet, arrange cookies with a floured spatula. Use sugar to sprinkle to your liking (or frost baked cookies after cooling). Put into the oven to bake at 375 degrees until light brown or for 8-10 minutes. Remove to wire rack to cool.

Nutrition Information

Calories: 94 calories Total Carbohydrate: 13g Cholesterol: 22 mg Total Fat: 4g Fiber: 0g Proteinr: 1g
Sodium: 86 mg

LITTLE PIGGY SUGAR COOKIES

Serving: about 4 dozen. **- Prep:** 15m **- Ready in:** 25m

INGREDIENTS

- 3/4 cup butter, softened
- 1 cup sugar
- 2 eggs
- 2 tbsps. milk
- 1/2 tsp. almond extract
- 3-1/4 cups all-purpose flour
- 2 tsps. baking powder
- Tinted frosting

DIRECTION

1. Cream sugar and butter in a big bowl till fluffy and light. Whip in milk, extract and eggs. Mix baking powder and flour; slowly put into creamed mixture and combine thoroughly. Chill with cover for 2 to 3 hours or till handleable.
2. Unroll dough on a slightly floured counter to thickness of 1/8-inch. Use a floured pig-shaped, 3-inches cookie cutter to cut dough out. Put on unoiled baking sheets, an-inch away.
3. Bake for about 7 to 9 minutes at 375° or till edges start to turn brown. Transfer onto wire racks and let cool. Use tinted icing to outline the cutouts.

Nutrition Information

Calories: 76 calories Total Carbohydrate: 11g Cholesterol: 17 mg Total Fat: 3g Fiber: 0g Proteinr: 1g
Sodium: 49 mg

MAPLE SUGAR COOKIES

Serving: 4 dozen. **- Prep:** 15m **- Ready in:** 25m

INGREDIENTS

- 1 cup butter-flavored shortening
- 1-1/4 cups sugar
- 2 eggs
- 1/4 cup maple syrup
- 3 tsps. vanilla extract
- 3 cups all-purpose flour
- 3/4 tsp. baking powder
- 1/2 tsp. baking soda
- 1/2 tsp. salt

DIRECTION

1. Cream sugar and shortening in a big bowl till fluffy and light. Put the eggs, one by one, whipping thoroughly after every increment. Whip in vanilla and syrup. Mix the rest of the ingredients; slowly put into creamed mixture and combine thoroughly. Chill with cover till handleable, for about 2 hours.
2. Unroll on a slightly floured counter into thickness of 1/8-inch. Use a 2-1/2-inches, floured cookie cutter to cut the dough. Arrange on unoiled baking sheets, an-inch away .
3. Bake for 9 to 12 minutes at 350° or till golden brown in color. Transfer onto wire racks and let cool.

Nutrition Information

Calories: 187 calories Total Carbohydrate: 25g Cholesterol: 18 mg Total Fat: 9g Fiber: 0g Proteinr: 2g Sodium: 94 mg

ORANGE SUGAR ROLLOUTS

Serving: about 3-1/2 dozen. **- Prep:** 25m **- Ready in:** 35m

INGREDIENTS

- 2/3 cup shortening
- 3/4 cup sugar
- 1 large egg
- 4 tsps. whole milk
- 1/2 to 1 tsp.grated orange zest
- 1/2 tsp. vanilla extract
- 2 cups all-purpose flour

- 1-1/2 tsps. baking powder
- 1/4 tsp. salt

FROSTING:

- 1/2 cup butter, softened
- 4 cups confectioners' sugar
- 1 tsp. vanilla extract
- 1/2 tsp.grated orange zest
- 2 to 4 tbsps. orange juice
- Yellow food coloring, optional

DIRECTION

1. Whisk together shortening and sugar in a large mixing bowl until fluffy and light. Beat in vanilla, orange zest, milk, and egg. Mix salt, baking powder, and flour together; slowly mix into creamed mixture.
2. Flatten dough to 1/4-inch thick on a work surface lightly coated with flour. Cut dough using 2 1/2-inch cookie cutters coated with flour. Arrange cookies 1 inch apart on oiled baking sheets. Bake for 6 to 8 minutes at 375° until lightly brown. Transfer cookies to wire racks and allow to cool.
3. Whisk butter, orange zest, vanilla, confectioners' sugar in a large mixing bowl with enough orange juice to reach spreading consistency. Mix in food coloring (if using). Spread on cooled cookies.

Nutrition Information

Calories: 260 calories Total Carbohydrate: 39g Cholesterol: 22 mg Total Fat: 11g Fiber: 0g Proteinr: 2g
Sodium: 105 mg

RED CHAPEAU SUGAR COOKIES

Serving: 5 dozen. - **Prep:** 45m - **Ready in:** 55m

INGREDIENTS

- 1 cup butter, softened
- 2 cups packed light brown sugar
- 2 eggs
- 2 tsps. lemon extract
- 4-1/2 cups all-purpose flour
- 1 tsp. baking soda
- 1/2 tsp. cream of tartar
- Red colored sugar or decorating frosting, optional

DIRECTION

1. Cream the butter and brown sugar in a large bowl. Beat in eggs and extract. Combine the cream of tartar, baking soda and flour; add to the creamed mixture little by little. Place inside the fridge, covered, for an hour or until easy to handle.

2. Split the dough into fourths. Lightly flour your work surface, then roll 1 portion to 1/8-in. thickness. Cut with a floured 6-in. hat-shaped cookie cutter. Arrange the dough 1 in. apart on ungreased baking sheets. Repeat with the rest of the dough.

3. Top it off with a sprinkle of red colored sugar if preferred. Bake inside the oven for 6-8 minutes at 350° or until edges start to brown. Transfer to wire racks to cool. Decorate with frosting if preferred.

Nutrition Information

Calories: 92 calories Total Carbohydrate: 14g Cholesterol: 15 mg Total Fat: 3g Fiber: 0g Proteinr: 1g Sodium: 57 mg

SMOOTH SAILING SUGAR COOKIES

Serving: about 4 dozen. **- Prep:** 30m **- Ready in:** 35m

INGREDIENTS

*   1 cup butter, softened
*   3/4 cup sugar
*   1 egg
*   2 tbsps. milk
*   1-1/2 tsps. vanilla extract
*   3 cups all-purpose flour
*   1 tsp. baking powder
*   1/2 tsp. salt

Frosting:

*   1 cup confectioners' sugar
*   1/2 tsp. vanilla or almond extract
*   1/4 tsp. salt
*   1 to 2 tbsps. milk
*   Food coloring, optional

DIRECTION

1. Cream sugar and butter in a big bowl till smooth. Whip in milk, vanilla and egg. Mix baking powder, salt and flour; slowly put to creamed mixture. Chill with cover for about an hour or till handleable.

2. Unroll dough on a slightly floured counter to thickness of 1/8-inch. Use your desire cookie cutters to cut dough. Put on oiled baking sheets 2-inches away. Bake about 5 to 8 minutes at 375° or till pale brown. Transfer onto the wire racks and let cool.

3. Mix salt, extract, confectioners' sugar and sufficient milk to attain spreading consistency in one small bowl. If wished, put in food coloring. Ice the cookies; jazz up as wished.

Nutrition Information

Calories: 172 calories Total Carbohydrate: 23g Cholesterol: 30 mg Total Fat: 8g Fiber: 0g Proteinr: 2g Sodium: 172 mg

SOUTH SEAS SUGAR COOKIES

Serving: about 2 dozen. **- Prep:** 40m **- Ready in:** 50m

INGREDIENTS

- 1/3 cup butter-flavored shortening
- 1/3 cup sugar
- 2/3 cup honey
- 1 egg
- 1 tsp. lemon extract
- 2-3/4 cups all-purpose flour
- 1 tsp. salt
- 1 tsp. baking soda

Frosting:

- 1/2 cup butter, softened
- 1/4 cup butter-flavored shortening
- 1/2 tsp. almond extract
- 1/8 tsp. salt
- 3-3/4 cups confectioners' sugar
- 3 to 4 tbsps. milk
- Yellow-gold, brown andgreen paste food coloring
- Yellow and orange colored sugar
- Chocolate chips

DIRECTION

1. Cream sugar and shortening in a big bowl till smooth. Whip in extract, egg and honey. Mix salt, baking soda and flour; slowly put into creamed mixture. Chill with cover for about 4 hours or till handleable.
2. Unroll dough on a slightly floured surface counter into thickness of 1/4-inch; use floured palm tree and pineapple cookie cutters to cut the dough. Arrange on oiled baking sheets, an-inch away. Bake for about 7 to 8 minutes at 375° or till set. Transfer onto wire racks and let cool.
3. For icing, whip confectioners' sugar, salt, extract, shortening and butter in small bowl till smooth; pour in sufficient milk to reach spreadable consistency. Color half cup brown, 2-1/2 cupsgreen and a cup of icing yellow-gold.
4. Ice tree trunks brown and pineapples yellow-gold. Trace lines on pineapples using toothpick; scatter colored sugar over.
5. Snip off a tiny hole in a plastic or pastry bag corner; fit a #21-star tip. Putgreen icing in bag; pipe leaves on palm trees and pineapples. For coconuts, put the chocolate chips onto palm trees.

SUGAR COOKIE SCARECROW AND PUMPKINS

Serving: 1 scarecrow and about 1 dozen pumpkins. **- Prep:** 45m **- Ready in:** 60m

INGREDIENTS

- 1 cup butter, softened
- 1-1/2 cups confectioners' sugar
- 1 large egg
- 1 tsp. almond extract
- 1 tsp. vanilla extract
- 2-1/2 cups all-purpose flour
- 1 tsp. baking soda
- 1 tsp. cream of tartar
- 4 tbsps. water
- Blue,green, red and yellow liquid or paste food coloring
- 3/4 cup vanilla frosting, divided
- Pastry tips- #18 open star and #5 round
- 1 largegreengumdrop, sliced into thirds
- 1 large redgumdrop, sliced into thirds

- 1 large blackgumdrop, sliced into fourths
- 1 yard thin ribbon, cut into 6 pieces

DIRECTION

1. Cream sugar and butter in a big bowl till fluffy and light. Put in the extracts and egg. Mix the dry ingredients; slowly put into creamed mixture and combine thoroughly. Chill with cover for 3 hours an up to overnight.
2. Form dough on a slightly floured counter into thickness of 1/4-inch. Slice into 2 squares 4-inch, 4 4x2-inch rectangles, 1 3x3/4-inch rectangle and 5x1-1/2-inch rectangle. Arrange together the 3-inch and 5-inch rectangles on unoiled baking sheet to make hat of scarecrow.
3. Put the rest of the pieces on unoiled baking sheets, 2-inches away. Round a 4-inches square's edges to make head of scarecrow. Create holes using a toothpick or straw so pieces of cookie can be attached with ribbon later, there should be a hole in every leg and arm, 5 holes on 4-inches body, 2 holes in the head and a hole in hat. Use a round, 2-1/2-inches cookie cutter to cut out the rest of the dough for pumpkin cookies. Arrange on unoiled baking sheets.
4. Bake for 12 to 15 minutes at 350° or till pale brown. Quickly transfer small round cookies onto wire racks and let cool. Open holes in pieces of scarecrow again using toothpick or straw. Cautiously transfer pieces of scarecrow onto wire racks.
5. Put 1 tbsp. of water into each of the 4-small bowls; color each with a variety of color of food coloring. Paint legs, body, arms and hat with small pastry brush. Mix yellow and red water to create orange. Paint round cookies withgreen - and orange -tinted water to look like pumpkins.
6. Color half cup of vanilla icing yellow. Snip off a small hole from corner of plastic or pastry bag; fit with a star tip. Put yellow frosting into the bag. Pipe straw on legs, arms, body and head. Stick pieces ofgumdrop with frosting to make patches, buttons, cheeks, nose and eyes.
7. Color the rest of frosting black. Prep another pastry or plastic bag, fit with round tip. Put black frosting into the bag. Pipe icing in a stitch design surrounding the mouth, patches and eyes. Dry the frosting for half an hour.
8. Put the pieces of scarecrow on board with cover; use ribbon to bind pieces together cautiously. Surround the scarecrow with pumpkins.

SUGARLESS HEART COOKIES

Serving: about 3 dozen. - **Prep:** 15m - **Ready in:** 25m

INGREDIENTS

- 3/4 cup butter, softened

- 1 package (.3 oz.) sugar-free raspberrygelatin
- 1/4 cup egg substitute
- 1 tsp. vanilla extract
- 1-3/4 cups all-purpose flour
- 1/2 tsp. baking powder

DIRECTION

1. Cream thegelatin and butter until fluffy and light in a small bowl. Beat in vanilla and egg substitute. Whisk baking powder and flour in a different bowl then beat into the creamed mixture gradually. Make a disk shape out of the dough then wrap with plastic. Put it in the refrigerator until firm enough to roll or for an hour.
2. Heat the oven beforehand to 400 degrees. Roll the dough to 1/4 inch thickness on a lightly floured surface. Cut it using a 1-3/4 inch floured heart-shaped cookie cutter ; put on baking sheets withoutgrease, leaving 1 inch space apart. Bake until bottoms are light brown and set or for 6 to 8 minutes. Allow it to cool by transfer to wire racks from pans.

Nutrition Information

Calories: 59 calories Total Carbohydrate: 5g Cholesterol: 0 mg Total Fat: 4g Fiber: 0g Proteinr: 1g Sodium: 49 mg

VALENTINE SUGAR COOKIES

Serving: 3-1/2 dozen. **- Prep:** 10m **- Ready in:** 20m

INGREDIENTS

- 1 cup butter, softened
- 1-1/2 cups confectioners' sugar
- 1 egg, lightly beaten
- 1 tsp. vanilla extract
- 1 tsp. almond extract
- 2-1/2 cups all-purpose flour
- Red decorator's sugar, optiona 1

DIRECTION

1. Cream the sugar and butter in a bowl. Put extracts and egg; mix in flour. Stir well then put in the refrigerator for several hours. Make 1/4-inch thickness dough by rolling on lightly floured surface. Slice

the dough using a 2 1/2 or 3-inch heart-shaped cookie cutter then put on baking sheets without grease. If desired, sprinkle sugar. Bake until lightly browned or for 8 to 10 minutes at 375 degrees.

Nutrition Information

Calories: 169 calories Total Carbohydrate: 20g Cholesterol: 33 mg Total Fat: 9g Fiber: 0g Proteinr: 2g Sodium: 91 mg

FROSTED BUTTER CUTOUTS

Serving: 5-1/2 dozen. - **Prep:** 30m - **Ready in:** 01h10m

INGREDIENTS

- 1/2 cup butter, softened
- 1 cup sugar
- 1 egg
- 1/2 cup sour cream
- 1 tsp. vanilla extract
- 3-1/2 cups all-purpose flour
- 1 tsp. baking soda
- 1/2 tsp. salt

Frosting:

- 1/4 cup cold milk
- 3 tbsps. instant vanilla pudding mix
- 1/4 cup butter, softened
- 2-1/2 cups confectioners' sugar
- 1 tsp. vanilla extract
- Food coloring, optional

DIRECTION

1. Cream sugar and butter together in a big bowl, then beat in vanilla, sour cream and egg. Mix together salt, baking soda and flour, then put into the creamed mixture gradually. Place on a cover and refrigerate for an hour, or until handle easily.
2. Roll out the dough on a work surface coated heavily with confectioners' sugar to the thickness of 1/8 inch. Use a 2 1/2 inch cookie cutter to cut the dough, then arrange on baking sheets coated with grease by 1 inch apart. Bake at 375 degrees until browned slightly, or for 8 to 10 minutes. Transfer to wire racks instantly to cool.

3. To make frosting, mix together pudding mix and milk until smooth, then put aside. Cream butter in a big bowl, then beat in pudding mixture. Put in food coloring, if wished, vanilla and confectioners' sugargradually, then beat on high speed until fluffy and light. Use the frosting to frost cookies.

FROSTED SOUR CREAM CUTOUTS

Serving: 5-1/2 dozen. **- Prep:** 30m **- Ready in:** 40m

INGREDIENTS

- 1/2 cup butter, softened
- 1 cup sugar
- 1 egg
- 1/2 cup sour cream
- 1 tsp. vanilla extract
- 3-1/2 cups all-purpose flour
- 1 tsp. baking soda
- 1/2 tsp. salt

Frosting:

- 1/4 cup cold milk
- 3 tbsps. instant vanilla pudding mix
- 1/4 cup butter, softened
- 2-1/2 cups confectioners' sugar
- 1 tsp. vanilla extract
- Food coloring, optional
- Edibleglitter

DIRECTION

1. Beat butter and sugar in a large mixing bowl. Beat in vanilla, sour cream, and egg. Mix salt, baking soda, and flour together; slow mix into creamed mixture. Refrigerate, covered, for 1 hour or until easy to work with.

2. Flatten dough to a thickness of 1/8 inch on a work surface heavily coated with confectioners' sugar. Cut dough using 2 1/2-inch cookie cutter. Arrange cookies 1 inch apart on buttered baking sheets. Bake for 8 to 10 minutes at 375° until lightly browned. Instantly transfer to wire racks to cool.

3. To make frosting, beat pudding mix and milk together until smooth; put to one side; beat butter in a large mixing bowl. Add pudding mixture and beat well. Slowly add vanilla, confectioners' sugar, and food coloring (if using); beat on high speed until fluffy and light. Pipe frosting onto cookies and garnish

with edibleglitter.

MOM'S OLD-FASHIONED CUTOUTS

Serving: 5 dozen. **- Prep:** 50m **- Ready in:** 60m

INGREDIENTS

- 1 cup butter, softened
- 1-1/2 cups sugar
- 1 large egg
- 1/2 cup sour cream
- 1 tsp. vanilla extract
- 4 cups all-purpose flour, sifted
- 1 tsp. baking powder
- 1/2 tsp. baking soda
- 1/2 tsp. salt
- 1/2 tsp.ground cinnamon orground nutmeg
- 2 cups confectioners' sugar
- 1 tsp. vanilla extract
- 1/4 tsp. salt
- 3 to 4 tbsps. heavy whipping cream
- Food coloring, optional

DIRECTION

1. Cream butter with sugar in a big bowl until fluffy and light. Whip in the egg, sour cream and vanilla. Combine the cinnamon, salt, baking soda, baking powder and flour in a separate bowl; whip into creamed mixturegradually.
2. Spit dough into 3 portions. Roll each into a disk; cover in plastic. Chill for 30 minutes or until easy to handle.
3. Shape each portion of dough to 1/4-in. thickness on a lightly floured surface. Slice with a floured 3-in. cookie cutter. Put 2 in. apart ongreased baking trays.
4. Bake for 10-12 minutes at 350° or until slightly browned. Take out to wire racks to cool completely.
5. Combine the salt, vanilla, confectioners' sugar and enough cream to reach desired consistency in a small bowl. Dye with food coloring (optional).garnish cookies as preferred.

PENGUIN CUTOUTS

Serving: 3 dozen. - **Prep:** 01h30m - **Ready in:** 01h40m

INGREDIENTS

- 1/2 cup butter-flavored shortening
- 1 cup sugar
- 1 egg
- 1-1/2 tsps. vanilla extract
- 1/2 cup sour cream
- 2-3/4 cups all-purpose flour
- 1/2 tsp. baking soda
- 1/2 tsp. salt

Frosting:

- 3-3/4 cups confectioners' sugar
- 1/3 cup water
- 4 tsps. meringue powder
- Orange, black and red and/orgreen paste food coloring

DIRECTION

1. Cream sugar and shortening in a big bowl till fluffy and light. Whip in vanilla and egg. Mix sour cream in. Mix baking soda, salt and flour; slowly put into creamed mixture and combine thoroughly. Split dough into 3 balls; chill with cover for 3 hours or till handleable.
2. Heat an oven to 375°. Take dough out of refrigerator, a portion at one time. Unroll dough on a slightly floured counter to thickness of 1/8-inch. Use a penguin-shaped, 4-inch, floured cookie cutter to cut dough. Arrange on unoiled baking sheets, an-inch apart.
3. Bake till edges turn pale brown, for 6 to 8 minutes. Transfer onto wire racks and let cool.
4. For icing, mix water, meringue powder and confectioners' sugar in small bowl; whip on low speed to just combine. Whip for 4 minutes on high to form soft peaks. Use plastic wrap or moist paper towels to cover icing between uses.
5. Put 1/2 of the icing aside. Color leftover 1/2 of frosting black. Split the rest of the frosting in half; color a portion orange and anothergreen and/or red.
6. Working briskly with black icing, pipe penguins' bodies outlines; fill in using thinned black icing. Allow to dry for a few hours at room temperature or till set. Fill in middles of penguins using thinned white icing; dry till set.
7. Use white and black icings for eyes, orange for feet and noses andgreen and/or red for scarves. Rest till

firm. Put white polka dots on scarves. Rest till firm. Keep in airtight container.

Nutrition Information

Calories: 139 calories Total Carbohydrate: 26g Cholesterol: 6 mg Total Fat: 4g Fiber: 0g Proteinr: 1g
Sodium: 56 mg

SOFT VALENTINE CUTOUTS

Serving: about 2 dozen. **- Prep:** 20m **- Ready in:** 30m

INGREDIENTS

- 1/2 cup butter, softened
- 1 cup sugar
- 1 egg
- 1/2 cup sour cream
- 1/4 tsp. lemon extract
- 1/4 tsp. vanilla extract
- 2 cups all-purpose flour
- 1/2 tsp. baking soda
- 1/8 tsp. salt
- Red colored sugar

DIRECTION

1. Beat sugar and butter in a large mixing bowl. Beat in extracts, sour cream, and egg. Mix salt, baking soda, and flour together; slowly mix into creamed mixture. Chill dough, covered, for 3 hours or until easy to work with.
2. Roll dough out to a 1/4 inch-thick on a work surface lightly coated with flour. Cut dough using a 2 1/2-inch heart-shaped cookie cutter coated with flour. Arrange cookies on ungreased baking sheets, separating them 1 inch apart. Scatter with colored sugar. Bake cookies for 8 to 10 minutes at 375° until lightly browned. Transfer to wire racks to cool.

Nutrition Information

Calories: 234 calories Total Carbohydrate: 33g Cholesterol: 45 mg Total Fat: 10g Fiber: 1g Proteinr: 3g
Sodium: 165 mg

SOUR CREAM CUTOUT COOKIES

Serving: about 3-1/2 dozen. **- Prep:** 25m **- Ready in:** 35m

INGREDIENTS

- 1 cup butter, softened
- 1-1/2 cups sugar
- 3 large eggs
- 1 cup sour cream
- 2 tsps. vanilla extract
- 3-1/2 cups all-purpose flour
- 2 tsps. baking powder
- 1 tsp. baking soda

Frosting:

- 1/3 cup butter, softened
- 2 cups confectioners' sugar
- 1-1/2 tsps. vanilla extract
- 1/4 tsp. salt
- 2 to 3 tbsps. whole milk

DIRECTION

1. Cream sugar and butter in a big bowl till fluffy and light. Whip eggs in. Put in the vanilla and sour cream; combine thoroughly. Whip baking powder, baking soda and flour in a separate bowl; slowly whip into creamed mixture. Split the dough in half. Fatten every portion into disk; encase using plastic. Chill for 2 hours or till set enough to roll.
2. Heat an oven to 350°. Form every dough portion on a thoroughly-floured counter into thickness of 1/4-inch. Use a 3-inch, floured cookie cutter to cut dough. Arrange on oiled baking sheets, 2-inches away.
3. Bake till tops bounce back once slightly pressed, for 10 to 12 minutes. Transfer from the pans onto wire racks and fully completely.
4. For icing, whip salt, vanilla, confectioners' sugar, butter, and sufficient milk in bowl to attain the preferred consistency. Smear on cookies.

Nutrition Information

Calories: 157 calories Total Carbohydrate: 21g Cholesterol: 34 mg Total Fat: 7g Fiber: 0g Proteinr: 2g Sodium: 111 mg

SOUR CREAM CUTOUTS

Serving: about 6-1/2 dozen. - **Prep:** 30m - **Ready in:** 45m

INGREDIENTS

- 1 cup butter, softened
- 2 cups sugar
- 3 egg s
- 1 cup (8 oz.) sour cream
- 1 tsp. vanilla extract
- 5-3/4 cups all-purpose flour
- 2 tsps. baking powder
- 1/2 tsp. baking soda
- 1/2 tsp. salt
- 2 cans (16 oz. each) vanilla frosting
- Gel food coloring of your choice

DIRECTION

1. Cream butter with sugar in a big bowl until fluffy and light. Whip in the vanilla, sour cream and eggs. Mix the salt, baking soda, baking powder and flour; put into creamed mixture gradually and stir well. Cover and chill overnight.
2. Shape dough to 1/8-in. thickness on a lightly floured surface. Slice with floured cookie cutters. Put 1 in. apart on ungreased baking trays. Bake for 12-15 minutes at 375° or until browned lightly. Take out to wire racks to cool.
3. Dye some of the frosting using food coloring; decorate cookies as you prefer.

Nutrition Information

Calories: 109 calories Total Carbohydrate: 16g Cholesterol: 17 mg Total Fat: 4g Fiber: 0g Proteinr: 1g Sodium: 73 mg

SUGAR-FREE MAPLE COOKIES

Serving: 42 cookies. - **Prep:** 10m - **Ready in:** 20m

INGREDIENTS

- 1/2 cup reduced-fat margarine, softened
- 1/2 cup sour cream
- 1 cup shredded peeled tart apple
- 2 eggs
- 1 tsp. maple flavoring
- 1/2 tsp. vanilla extract
- 2 cups all-purpose flour
- Artificial brown sugar sweetener equivalent to 1/3 cup brown sugar
- 1/2 tsp. baking soda
- 1/2 tsp. baking powder

DIRECTION

1. Mix together vanilla, maple flavoring, eggs, apple, sour cream and margarine in a bowl. Mix baking powder, baking soda, sweetener and flour, then put into the apple mixture, mixing well.
2. Drop onto baking sheets sprayed with cooking spray with heaping tablespoonfuls of batter. Bake at 375 degrees until brown slightly, about 9 to 10 minutes. Allow to cool on wire racks then put in an airtight container for storage.

Nutrition Information

Calories: 44 calories Total Carbohydrate: 5g Cholesterol: 11 mg Total Fat: 2g Fiber: 0g Proteinr: 1g Sodium: 51 mg

WATERMELON SUGAR COOKIES

Serving: about 8-1/2 dozen. - **Prep:** 30m - **Ready in:** 40m

INGREDIENTS

- 1 cup butter, softened
- 1-1/2 cups sugar
- 2 large eggs
- 1 tsp. vanilla extract
- 3 cups all-purpose flou r
- 1 tsp. baking soda
- 1/2 tsp. salt
- 1 cup sour cream

- 1 can (12 oz.) whipped vanilla frosting
- Red andgreen food coloring
- Miniature chocolate chips

DIRECTION

1. Beat together sugar and butter in a large mixing bowl until fluffy and light. Beat in vanilla and eggs. Mix salt, baking soda, and flour together; slowly mix alternately with sour cream into the creamed mixture, mixing well between additions. Chill dough, covered, for 2 hours or overnight.
2. Flatten half of the dough to 1/8-inch thickness on a work surface heavily coated with flour. Use a 3-inch round cookie cutter to cut dough into circles; cut circles in half. Do the same with the rest of dough.
3. Arrange cookies on ungreased baking sheets. Bake for 9 to 10 minutes at 375° or until cookies are firm and bottoms turn brown lightly. Allow cookies to cool on wire racks.
4. Put 2/3 of the frosting into a mixing bowl; mix in red food coloring. Mixgreen food coloring into the rest of frosting. Scatter on tops of cookies with pink frosting. Using a pastry bag with a tiny star tip if wanted, frost edges withgreen frosting. Scatter chocolate chips randomly over the pink frosting for seeds.

Nutrition Information

Calories: 122 calories Total Carbohydrate: 16g Cholesterol: 21 mg Total Fat: 6g Fiber: 0g Proteinr: 1g Sodium: 103 mg

AMISH SUGAR COOKIES

Serving: 72 - **Prep:** 15m - **Ready in:** 25m

INGREDIENTS

- 1 1/2 cups vegetable oil
- 1 1/2 cups white sugar
- 2 eggs
- 4 cups all-purpose flour
- 1 tsp. baking soda
- 1 tsp. baking powder
- 1 cup buttermilk
- 3/4 tsp. salt
- 3/4 tsp. vanilla extract

DIRECTION

1. Preheat the oven to 175 degrees C (350 degrees F).
2. Combine together eggs, sugar, and vegetable oil (about 1 1/2 cups of vegetable oil). Stir in flour, vanilla, baking soda, buttermilk, baking powder and salt.
3. Transfer the batter onto cookie sheets by tsp.-sized amounts and leave plenty of room in between. The cookies will puff up and become large.
4. Bake for about 8 to 10 minutes .

Nutrition Information

Calories: 85 calories; Total Carbohydrate: 9.7g Cholesterol: 5 mg Total Fat: 4.8g Proteinr: 1g Sodium: 54 mg

BROWN SUGAR CRINKLES

Serving: about 13 dozen. **- Prep:** 20m **- Ready in:** 30m

INGREDIENTS

- 1 cup butter, softened
- 1 cup shortening
- 3 cups sugar
- 1-1/2 cups packed brown sugar
- 6 eggs
- 1 tbsp. vanilla extract
- 6 cups all-purpose flour
- 1 tbsp. baking soda
- 1-1/2 tsps. salt

DIRECTION

1. Beat sugars, shortening and butter in a big bowl. Put in eggs, 1 at a time, mixing thoroughly between additions. Mix in vanilla. Mix together salt, baking soda and flour; pour little by little into the beaten mixture to make the soft dough.
2. Scoop dough by rounded teaspoonfuls and place on ungreased baking sheets, laying each 2 inches away from others. Use aglass coated with sugar to flatten the dough. Bake in 350-degree oven until light brown, about 10-12 minutes. Allow to cool for two minutes then transfer to wire racks.

Calories: 130 calories Total Carbohydrate: 19g Cholesterol: 23 mg Total Fat: 5g Fiber: 0g Proteinr: 1g
Sodium: 124 mg

BROWN SUGAR ICEBOX COOKIES

Serving: about 3-1/2 dozen. **- Prep:** 15m **- Ready in:** 25m

INGREDIENTS

- 1/2 cup butter, softened
- 1 cup packed brown sugar
- 1 large egg
- 1 tsp. vanilla extract
- 1-3/4 cups all-purpose flour
- 1/2 tsp. baking soda
- 1/4 tsp. salt
- 2/3 cup chopped pecans or sweetened shredded coconut

DIRECTION

1. Whip the butter with sugar in a big bowl. Put in the vanilla and egg; stir well. Mix the salt, baking soda and flour; put into cream mixture gradually. Fold in coconut or pecans (dough will be sticky). Roll into 2 rolls; wrap in plastic wrap individually. Chill for 4 hours or overnight.
2. Unwrap and slice into 1/4-in. slices. Put 2 in. apart on ungreased baking trays. Bake 7 to 10 minutes at 375° or until firm. Take out to wire racks.

Nutrition Information

Calories: 146 calories Total Carbohydrate: 19g Cholesterol: 22 mg Total Fat: 7g Fiber: 1g Proteinr: 2g
Sodium: 109 mg

BROWN SUGAR SHORTBREAD

Serving: 36

INGREDIENTS

- 8 oz. unsalted butter at room temperature

- 1/2 tsp. Diamond Crystal Kosher Salt
- 3 1/2 oz. dark brown sugar
- 8 oz. all-purpose flour
- Demerara, turbinado, or other coarse sugar, as needed
- Diamond Crystal Coarse Sea Salt, as needed

DIRECTION

1. Use an electric mixer to cream together the dark brown sugar, Diamond Crystal(R) Kosher Salt and butter in a bowl for 5 minutes on high speed. Add flour to the mixture and mix on low speed until just incorporated.
2. Scrape the dough onto a parchment paper sheet; shape it into a 2 inch diameter log. Use the parchment paper to wrap it. Refrigerate until thoroughly chilled, about an hour.
3. Set oven to preheat at 350°F (175°C).grease cookie sheets lightly with oil.
4. Take the dough out of the parchment and roll it into demerara sugar to evenly coat. Cut it into rounds with the thickness of 1/4 inch and place them onto cookie sheets.
5. Sprinkle each cookie with a pinch of Diamond Crystal(R) Coarse Sea Salt and more demerara sugar.
6. Bake till very light brown and firm when touched, about 8 to 10 minutes.

Nutrition Information

Calories: 78 calories; Total Carbohydrate: 7.5g Cholesterol: 13 mg Total Fat: 5.1g Proteinr: 0.7g Sodium: 40 mg

CINNAMON-SUGAR CRISPS

Serving: 3-1/2 dozen. **- Prep:** 30m **- Ready in:** 45m

INGREDIENTS

- 3/4 cup butter, softened
- 1/3 cup sugar
- 1/3 cup packed brown sugar
- 1 large egg
- 1 tsp. vanilla extract
- 1-3/4 cups all-purpose flour
- 1 tsp.ground cinnamon
- 1/4 tsp. salt
- 2 tbsps. colored sprinkles

DIRECTION

1. Cream sugars and butter in a big bowl till fluffy and light. Whip in vanilla and egg. Mix cinnamon, salt and flour; slowly put into creamed mixture and combine thoroughly. Form into a roll of 12-inches; encase using plastic. Chill till set, about 2 hours.
2. Remove the wrap and slice to half-inch pieces. Put on unoiled baking sheets spacing 2-inches apart. Use sprinkles to jazz up.
3. Bake about 10 to 12 minutes at 350° or till pale brown. Transfer onto wire racks and let cool.

Nutrition Information

Calories: 66 calories Total Carbohydrate: 8g Cholesterol: 14 mg Total Fat: 4g Fiber: 0g Proteinr: 1g Sodium: 50 mg

CRISP ALMOND SUGAR COOKIES

Serving: 5 dozen. **- Prep:** 15m **- Ready in:** 25m

INGREDIENTS

- 2 cups butter-flavored shortening
- 1 cup sugar
- 1 cup packed brown sugar
- 2 eggs
- 1 tsp. vanilla extract
- 1 tsp. almond extract
- 4 cups all-purpose flour
- 2 tsps. baking soda
- 2 tsps. cream of tartar
- Additional sugar or colored sugar

DIRECTION

1. Whisk sugars and shortening together in a large mixing bowl until fluffy and light. Put in eggs, one by one, beating well between additions. Add extracts and beat well. Mix together cream of tartar, baking soda, and flour; slowly mix into creamed mixture until well combined.
2. Drop mixture onto ungreased baking sheets by tablespoonfuls, separating them 2 inches apart. Press cookies using aglass dipped in sugar. Bake for 10 to 12 minutes at 350° until lightly brown. Transfer cookies to wire rack to cool.

Nutrition Information

Calories: 238 calories Total Carbohydrate: 27g Cholesterol: 14 mg Total Fat: 13g Fiber: 0g Proteinr: 2g
Sodium: 91 mg

CRISP LEMON SUGAR COOKIES

Serving: about 6-1/2 dozen. **- Prep:** 15m **- Ready in:** 25m

INGREDIENTS

- 1/2 cup butter, softened
- 1/2 cup butter-flavored shortening
- 1 cup sugar
- 1 egg
- 1 tbsp. milk
- 2 tsps. lemon extract
- 1 tsp. vanilla extract
- 2-1/2 cups all-purpose flour
- 3/4 tsp. salt
- 1/2 tsp. baking soda
- Additional sugar

DIRECTION

1. Whisk sugar, shortening, and butter together in a large mixing bowl until fluffy and light. Beat in extracts, milk, and egg. Mix baking soda, salt, and flour together; slowly mix into creamed mixture.
2. Form dough into 1-inch balls or drop by rounded teaspoonfuls about 2 inches apart onto unbuttered baking sheets. Press balls using aglass dipped in sugar.
3. Bake cookies for 9 to 11 minutes at 400° until edges turn brown lightly. Instantly transfer cookies to wire rack and let them cool.

Nutrition Information

Calories: 96 calories Total Carbohydrate: 11g Cholesterol: 12 mg Total Fat: 5g Fiber: 0g Proteinr: 1g
Sodium: 87 mg

GIANT LEMON SUGAR COOKIES

Serving: 14 cookies. **- Prep:** 25m **- Ready in:** 40m

INGREDIENTS

- 1 cup unsalted butter, softened
- 1-1/2 cups sugar
- 1/2 cup packed brown sugar
- 2 large eggs
- 1-1/2 tsps.grated lemon peel
- 2 tbsps. lemon juice
- 3 cups all-purpose flour
- 1 tsp. baking soda
- 1/4 tsp. salt
- 1/4 tsp. cream of tartar
- 4 tsps. coarse sugar

DIRECTION

1. Prepare the oven by preheating to 350 degrees F. Cream sugars and butter in a large bowl until fluffy and light in weight. Add in eggs. Mix in juice and lemon peel. In a separate bowl, mix cream of tartar, salt, baking soda and flour; slowly mix into the creamed mixture. Form 1/4 cupfuls of dough into balls. Ongreased baking sheets, place them 6 inches apart. Use bottom of measuring cup to flatten to 3/4 inches thickness. Slightly sweep tops with water; drizzle with coarse sugar. Place inside the preheated oven for 12-15 minutes or until light brown in color. Then separate from pans and put on wire racks to let cool fully. Use airtight containers to store.

Nutrition Information

Calories: 340 calories Total Carbohydrate: 51g Cholesterol: 65 mg Total Fat: 14g Fiber: 1g Proteinr: 4g Sodium: 147 mg

LEMON SUGAR COOKIES

Serving: about 11 dozen. **- Prep:** 20m **- Ready in:** 30m

INGREDIENTS

* 1 cup butter, softened
* 1 cup sugar
* 1 cup confectioners' sugar
* 1 cup canola oil
* 2 eggs
* 1 tsp. lemon extract
* 4-1/2 cups all-purpose flour
* 1 tsp. baking soda
* 1 tsp. cream of tartar
* Additional sugar

DIRECTION

2. Set oven to 350° to preheat. Beat sugars and butter together in a large mixing bowl until incorporated. Beat in extract and eggs. Combine cream of tartar, baking soda, and flour; beat into butter mixture until dough becomes stiff.
3. Shape dough into balls about 1 inch in diameter; arrange cookies 2 inches apart on ungreased baking sheets. Flatten cookies using the bottom of a glass dipped in water, then in sugar. Bake cookies in the preheated oven until edges turn brown lightly, for 10 minutes.

Nutrition Information

Calories: 106 calories Total Carbohydrate: 11g Cholesterol: 14 mg Total Fat: 6g Fiber: 0g Proteinr: 1g Sodium: 49 mg

NUTTY SUGAR CRISPS

Serving: 8-1/2 dozen. - **Prep:** 15m - **Ready in:** 25m

INGREDIENTS

* 1 cup butter, softened
* 1/2 cup vegetable oil
* 1 cup sugar
* 1 cup confectioners' sugar
* 2 eggs
* 1 tsp. vanilla extract
* 4-1/2 cups all-purpose flour

- 1 tsp. baking soda
- 1 tsp. cream of tartar
- 1 cup chopped walnuts

DIRECTION

1. Cream oil, sugars and butter in one bowl, till fluffy and light. Put in the eggs, one by one, whipping thoroughly after every increment. Whip vanilla in. Mix baking soda, cream of tartar and flour; slowly put into creamed mixture. Mix walnuts in.
2. Drop on unoiled baking sheets, by teaspoonfuls, spacing 2-inches away. Use oneglass dipped in sugar to flatten a bit. Bake for about 10 to 12 minutes at 375° or till edges turngolden brown in color. Transfer onto wire racks and let cool.

Nutrition Information

Calories: 133 calories Total Carbohydrate: 15g Cholesterol: 18 mg Total Fat: 7g Fiber: 0g Proteinr: 2g Sodium: 64 mg

PUDDING SUGAR COOKIES

Serving: 7 dozen. **- Prep:** 15m **- Ready in:** 30m

INGREDIENTS

- 1 cup butter, softened
- 1 cup canola oil
- 1 cup sugar
- 1 cup confectioners' sugar
- 2 eggs
- 1 tsp. vanilla extract
- 1 package (3.4 oz.) instant lemon pudding mix or instant pudding mix of your choice
- 4 cups all-purpose flour
- 1 tsp. cream of tartar
- 1 tsp. baking soda

DIRECTION

1. Whisk butter with sugars and oil in a large mixing bowl until fluffy and light. Whisk in dry pudding mix, vanilla, and eggs. Mix baking soda, cream of tartar, and flour together; slowly mix into creamed mixture until incorporated.

2. Drop batter onto ungreased baking sheets by tablespoonfuls, separating them 2 inches apart. Press each mound with aglass dipped in sugar.

3. Bake cookies for 12 to 15 minutes at 350° until lightly browned. Transfer cookies to wire racks.

Nutrition Information

Calories: 169 calories Total Carbohydrate: 19g Cholesterol: 22 mg Total Fat: 10g Fiber: 0g Proteinr: 2g Sodium: 105 mg

QUILTED SUGAR COOKIES

Serving: about 3 dozen. - **Prep:** 25m - **Ready in:** 45m

INGREDIENTS

- 3/4 cup butter, softened
- 1/3 cup confectioners' sugar
- 2 tbsps. sugar
- 1 large egg
- 1-1/2 cups all-purpose flour
- 1/2 cup vanilla frosting and food coloring or decorator's icing

DIRECTION

1. Beat together sugar and butter in a bowl. Put in eggs; mix thoroughly. Put in flour; stir thoroughly. Let it chill with cover for at least one hour. Use heavy duty foil to line a 15x10x1-inch baking pan. Force dough onto pan's bottom. Use a sharp knife to score dough making squares of 2x2-inches (reroll scraps and bake as directed orget rid of it). Put into the oven to bake at 325 degrees until set or for 16 to 18 minutes. The cookies will not turn brown. Use foil to take the cookies off the pan carefully. Slice into squares and let it cool. Use decorator's icing or stir food coloring into frosting to create preferred colors. Use quilt patterns to decorate cookies.

Nutrition Information

Calories: 156 calories Total Carbohydrate: 17g Cholesterol: 32 mg Total Fat: 9g Fiber: 0g Proteinr: 2g Sodium: 96 mg

SMILING SUGAR COOKIES

Serving: about 2 dozen. - **Prep:** 30m - **Ready in:** 40m

INGREDIENTS

- 1/2 cup butter, softened
- 1/2 cup sugar
- 1/2 cup packed brown sugar
- 1 egg
- 1/3 cup 2% milk
- 2 tsps. vanilla extract
- 3 cups all-purpose flour
- 2 tsps. cream of tartar
- 1 tsp. baking soda
- 1/2 tsp. salt
- About 24 Popsicle sticks
- 1 cup vanilla frosting
- Red, blue andgreen paste food coloring
- Assorted small candies

DIRECTION

1. Turn on the oven to 375 degrees to preheat. Beat together sugars and butter in a large bowl until fluffy and light. Whip in vanilla, milk and egg. Mix together salt, baking soda, cream of tartar and flour; put to creamed mixture slowly and mix thoroughly. Form dough into balls of 1 1/2 inches; use a wooden pop stick to insert in the center of each one.

2. Arrange on lightlygreased baking sheets 2 inches apart; slightly flatten. Put into the oven to bake until lightly brown, for 8 to 10 minutes. Transfer on wire racks to cool. In three bowls, distribute frosting; color to your liking. In resealable plastic bags, add every frostings of different color; make a small hole in the corner of the bag. Pipe mouths and hair on the cookies; attach small candies for eyes using a dap of frosting. Allow to dry for 30 minutes at least.

Nutrition Information

Calories: 180 calories Total Carbohydrate: 29 g Cholesterol: 20 mg Total Fat: 6g Fiber: 0g Proteinr: 2g
Sodium: 170 mg

SUGAR COOKIE SLICES

Serving: 5 dozen. **- Prep:** 10m **- Ready in:** 25m

INGREDIENTS

- 1-1/2 cups butter, softened
- 1-1/2 cups sugar
- 1/2 tsp. vanilla extract
- 3 cups all-purpose flour
- 1 tsp. baking soda
- 1/2 tsp. salt

DIRECTION

1. Cream together sugar and butter in a large bowl until fluffy and light. Add vanilla and beat well. Mix salt, baking soda, and flour together; slowly mix into creamed mixture.
2. Form mixture into 2 rolls approximately 8 inches in diameter; use plastic wrap to wrap each roll. Chill until hardened, for 4 hours.
3. Remove wrap, slice into 1/4-inch slices. Lay cookies on ungreased baking sheets, separating them 2 inches apart. Bake cookies for 12 to 14 minutes at 350° until firm but not browned. Transfer cookies to wire racks and allow to cool.

Nutrition Information

Calories: 165 calories Total Carbohydrate: 20g Cholesterol: 25 mg Total Fat: 9g Fiber: 0g Proteinr: 1g Sodium: 174 mg

SUGARGEMS

Serving: about 7 dozen. **- Prep:** 20m **- Ready in:** 35m

INGREDIENTS

- 1 cup shortening
- 1 cup vegetable oil
- 1 cup sugar
- 1 cup confectioners' sugar
- 2 eggs
- 1 tsp. vanilla extract
- 4-1/2 cups all-purpose flour
- 1 tsp. baking soda
- 1 tsp. cream of tartar
- 1/2 tsp. salt

- Additional sugar or colored sugar

DIRECTION

1. Cream oil, sugars and shortening in a big bowl till fluffy and light. Put the eggs, one by one, whipping thoroughly after every increment. Whip vanilla in. Mix salt, cream of tartar, baking soda and flour; slowly put into creamed mixture. Chill with cover for an hour or till handleable.
2. Form into an-inch rounds; dip surfaces in colored sugar or sugar. Put on unprepped baking sheets, 2-inches away, sugar side facing up. Bake for 12 to 14 minutes at 350° or till edges start to turn brown. Transfer onto wire racks and let cool.

Nutrition Information

Calories: 170 calories Total Carbohydrate: 18g Cholesterol: 10 mg Total Fat: 10g Fiber: 0g Proteinr: 2g Sodium: 61 mg

SUGARY DESSERT SHELLS

Serving: 8 servings. **- Prep:** 20m **- Ready in:** 30m

INGREDIENTS

- 2 egg whites
- 1/2 cup sugar
- 1/4 cup butter, melted
- 1/2 tsp. vanilla extract
- 1/2 cup all-purpose flour
- Pudding, mousse or ice cream
- Fresh fruit

DIRECTION

1. Use parchment paper to line a baking sheet. On the paper, draw2 6-inch circles; set aside. Beat egg whites in a small bowl on medium speed until it forms soft peaks. Beat in sugargradually, a tbsp. at one time, on high until it forms stiff peaks. Whip in vanilla and butter. Whip in flourgradually until smooth.
2. On each parchment paper circle, scoop 2 tbsps. of batter; use the back of the spoon to spread to cover the circle. Put into the oven to bake at 350 degrees until the edges are lightly brown or for 8 to 9 minutes.
3. Use a mental spatula to remove from the paper and transfer each into a small bowl or an inverted 6-oz. custard cup immediately to and shape around the cup. Redo with the rest of the batter to make six additional shells. You can reuse parchment paper. Fill with fruit and pudding.

Nutrition Information

Calories: 132 calories Total Carbohydrate: 19g Cholesterol: 15 mg Total Fat: 6g Fiber: 0g Proteinr: 2g
Sodium: 72 mg

SWEET-AS-SUGAR COOKIES

Serving: about 5 dozen. **- Prep:** 25m **- Ready in:** 35m

INGREDIENTS

- 1 cup butter, softened
- 1 cup sugar
- 1 cup confectioners' sugar
- 1 cup vegetable oil
- 2 large eggs
- 4-1/4 cups all-purpose flour
- 1 tsp. salt
- 1 tsp. cream of tartar
- 1 tsp. baking soda
- 1 tsp. vanilla extract
- Additional sugar
- Nutmeg

DIRECTION

1. Cream sugars, oil and butter in bowl. Put the eggs, one by one, whipping thoroughly after every increment. Put the vanilla and dry ingredients; combine thoroughly. Chill the dough overnight.
2. Shape into balls with the size of walnut and arrange on oiled baking sheets. Mix nutmeg and sugar; in the mixture, dip theglass and use it to flatten the cookies. Bake for about 8 minutes at 375°. Allow to cool onto wire rack.

Nutrition Information

Calories: 229 calories Total Carbohydrate: 24g Cholesterol: 31 mg Total Fat: 14g Fiber: 0g Proteinr: 2g
Sodium: 187 mg

VINEGAR SUGAR COOKIE S

Serving: 3-1/2 dozen. **- Prep:** 35m **- Ready in:** 45m

INGREDIENTS

- 1 cup butter, softened
- 3/4 cup sugar
- 1 tbsp. white vinegar
- 1/2 tsp. vanilla extract
- 2 cups all-purpose flour
- 1 tsp. baking soda
- Colored sugar

DIRECTION

1. Beat together sugar and butter in a large bowl until fluffy and light. Whip in vanilla and vinegar. Mix together baking soda and flour; put to creamed mixture slowly and blend thoroughly.
2. Form into balls of 1-inch. Ongreased baking sheets, arrange 2 inches apart from each other. Flatten until they are 1/4-inch thick; scatter colored sugar over.
3. Put into the oven to bake at 350 degrees until edges are light brown or for 8 to 10 minutes. Allow to cool for 1 minute before transfer to wire racks. Put into an airtight container to store.

Nutrition Information
Calories: 74 calories Total Carbohydrate: 8g Cholesterol: 11 mg Total Fat: 4g Fiber: 0g Proteinr: 1g
Sodium: 61 mg

EASY SOFT SUGAR COOKIES

Serving: about 6 dozen. **- Prep:** 15m **- Ready in:** 25m

INGREDIENTS

- 1 cup butter, softened
- 2-1/4 cups sugar, divided
- 2 eggs
- 5 cups all-purpose flour
- 1 tsp. baking soda

- 1/2 tsp. baking powder
- 1-1/2 tsps.ground cardamom, divided
- 1/2 cup milk

DIRECTION

1. Cream 2 cups sugar and butter in a big bowl. Put the eggs, one by one, whipping thoroughly after every increment. Mix a tsp. cardamom, baking powder, baking soda and flour; put into creamed mixture alternating with the milk. Mix cardamom and the leftover sugar in one small bowl; dredge a rounded teaspoonfuls dough into mixture of sugar. Arrange on oiled baking sheets. Bake for about 10 to 12 minutes at 375° or till pale brown. Transfer on wire racks to cool.

Nutrition Information

Calories: 163 calories Total Carbohydrate: 26g Cholesterol: 26 mg Total Fat: 6g Fiber: 0 g Proteinr: 2g Sodium: 98 mg

SOFT SUGAR COOKIE

Serving: about 6-1/2 dozen. **- Prep:** 10m **- Ready in:** 20m

INGREDIENTS

- 3/4 cup shortening
- 1-1/2 cups sugar
- 2 eggs
- 1 tsp. vanilla extract
- 3 cups all-purpose flour
- 2 tsps. baking powder
- 1 tsp. baking soda
- 1/2 tsp. salt
- 1 cup buttermilk
- Raisins

DIRECTION

1. Cream sugar and shortening in a big bowl, till fluffy and light. Put eggs, one by one, whipping thoroughly after every increment. Whip vanilla in. Mix salt, baking soda, baking powder and flour; put into creamed mixture alternating with buttermilk, whipping thoroughly after every increment. Chill with cover for not less than 2 hours, till dough is extremely soft.

2. Drop tablespoonfuls of dough on unoiled baking sheets, spacing 2-inches apart. Put one a raisin in the middle of every cookie. Bake about 8 to 10 minutes at 375° or till pale brown. Transfer onto wire racks and let cool.

Nutrition Information

Calories: 105 calories Total Carbohydrate: 15g Cholesterol: 11 mg Total Fat: 4g Fiber: 0g Proteinr: 2g Sodium: 93 mg

AMAZING SUGAR COOKIES

Serving: 48 - **Prep:** 15m - **Ready in:** 40m

INGREDIENTS

- 2 3/4 cups all-purpose flour
- 1 tsp. baking soda
- 1/2 tsp. baking powder
- 1 cup butter, softened
- 1 1/2 cups white sugar
- 1 egg
- 1 tsp. vanilla extract
- 1/4 cup white sugar

DIRECTION

1. Heat an oven to 190 ° C or 375 ° F.
2. In one small bowl, combine baking soda, baking powder and flour.
3. Into a big bowl, whip 1 1/2 cups sugar and butter using electric mixer till smooth; mix in vanilla extract and egg. Slowly mix flour mixture into mixture of butter. Form the dough into balls the size of walnut and toss in quarter cup of sugar; arrange on unprepped baking sheets, 2-inch away .
4. Bake for 8 to 9 minutes in prepped oven tillgolden. Rest for 2 minutes on cookie sheet then remove to wire racks and let cool.

Nutrition Information

Calories: 90 calories; Total Carbohydrate: 12.8g Cholesterol: 14 mg Total Fat: 4g Proteinr: 0.9g Sodium: 60 mg

AMISH SUGAR CAKES

Serving: 30 - **Prep:** 15m - **Ready in:** 30m

INGREDIENTS

- 1 cup butter flavored shortening
- 2 cups white sugar
- 3 eggs
- 1 1/2 tsps. vanilla extract
- 3 1/2 cups all-purpose flour
- 1 tbsp. baking powder
- 1 tsp. baking soda
- 1 tsp. cream of tartar
- 1 pinch salt
- 1 cup buttermilk
- 1/4 cup white sugar

DIRECTION

1. Preheat the oven to 175 degrees C (350 degrees F). Coat cookie sheets withgrease.
2. Cream together two cups of sugar and shortening in a large bowl until smooth. Mix in eggs, one by one and add vanilla. Mix the flour, cream of tartar, baking powder, salt and baking soda. Mix into the creamed mixture alternating with buttermilk until the resulting mix is blended well. Transfer large heaping tablespoonfuls onto the prepared cookie sheets placing approximately three inches apart. Drizzle some of the remaining sugar onto each cookie.
3. Bake in the preheated oven for about 10 to 12 minutes until the edges start to becomegolden. Transfer from the baking sheets to wire racks to cool. Once cool, keep in an airtight container.

Nutrition Information

Calories: 186 calories; Total Carbohydrate: 26.7g Cholesterol: 19 mg Total Fat: 7.9g Proteinr: 2.4g Sodium: 97 mg

ANGEL COOKIES I

Serving: 96

INGREDIENTS

- 1 cup butter
- 1 cup lard
- 1 cup white sugar
- 1 cup packed brown sugar
- 2 tsps. salt
- 2 eggs
- 2 tsps. vanilla extract
- 4 1/2 cups all-purpose flour
- 2 tsps. baking soda
- 2 tsps. cream of tartar
- 1 cup chopped walnuts

DIRECTION

1. Beat butter, sugars, and lard together. Mix in eggs, one by one, until well combined. Add dry ingredients and vanilla; fold in chopped nuts.
2. Refrigerate dough until easy to handle.
3. Form dough into balls and press into sugar to coat. Bake cookies for approximately 20 minutes at 350°F (175°C) .

Nutrition Information

Calories: 84 calories; Total Carbohydrate: 9g Cholesterol: 11 mg Total Fat: 5g Proteinr: 0.9g Sodium: 91 mg

ANISE SEED BORRACHIO COOKIES

Serving: 36 **- Prep:** 25m **- Ready in:** 35m

INGREDIENTS

- 2 tbsps. anise seed
- 3 tbsps. rum
- 1 1/4 cups butter
- 3/4 cup white sugar
- 1 1/2 tsps. vanilla extract
- 2 1/2 cups all-purpose flour

- 1 egg
- 1/2 tsp. salt
- 1 tsp. baking powder
- 1 1/2 tsps.ground cloves

DIRECTION

1. In a small bowl, place anise seeds with rum. Put aside and let marinate overnight.
2. Cream vanilla, sugar and butter together in a medium bowl till smooth. Add in rum and anise seeds then stir. Mix in egg. Combine cloves, baking powder, salt and flour then place into the butter mixture; stir to blend well. Cover then store for 1 hour in the fridge.
3. Preheat the oven to 175°C or 350°F. Roll out the dough into 1/8-in. thick on a surface that has been lightly floured. Use cookie cutters to cut into shapes you desire. Put the cookies on a cookie sheet that has beengreased.
4. Bake in the preheat oven for 10 minutes till the edges aregolden brown. Let cool on baking sheets for a few minutes then transfer onto wire racks to completely cool.

Nutrition Information

Calories: 111 calories; Total Carbohydrate: 11.1g Cholesterol: 22 mg Total Fat: 6.7g Proteinr: 1.2g Sodium: 90 mg

BACHELOR BUTTONS II

Serving: 36 - **Prep:** 20m - **Ready in:** 32m

INGREDIENTS

- 2 cups all-purpose flour
- 3/4 tsp. salt
- 1 tsp. baking soda
- 3/4 cup shortening
- 1 cup packed brown sugar
- 1 egg
- 1 tsp. vanilla extract

DIRECTION

1. Heat an oven to 190 ° C or 375 ° F. Oil the cookie sheets. Sift salt, baking soda and flour together, put aside.

2. Cream brown sugar and shortening in medium bowl till smooth. Whip in vanilla and egg. Mix sifted ingredients in to blend thoroughly. Form dough into balls of 3/4 inch or small crescents. Put the cookies on prepped cookie sheet 2-inch away.

3. Bake in prepped oven, about 8 to 10 minutes. Cool cookies for 5 minutes on baking sheet then transfer onto a wire rack to fully cool.

Nutrition Information

Calories: 89 calories; Total Carbohydrate: 11.3 g Cholesterol: 5 mg Total Fat: 4.5g Proteinr: 0.9g Sodium: 87 mg

BANANA PUDDING SUGAR COOKIES

Serving: 30 - **Prep:** 15m - **Ready in:** 2h35m

INGREDIENTS

- 2/3 cup shortening
- 2/3 cup white sugar
- 2 eggs
- 1 tsp. vanilla extract
- 1/2 tsp. baking powder
- 1/2 tsp. salt
- 1 (3.5 oz.) package instant banana pudding mix
- 2 1/2 cups all-purpose flour

DIRECTION

1. Cream sugar and shortening together in a medium bowl until fluffy and light. Beat in 1 egg at a time, then stir in instant banana pudding mix, salt, baking powder and vanilla extract. Mix in 2 cups of flour, then mix in leftover 1/2 cup of flourgradually as necessary to make a workable dough. Cover dough and refrigerate in the fridge for a minimum of 2 hours.

2. Set the oven to 190°C or 375°F to preheat. Coat baking sheets withgrease. Form dough into balls with walnut size and arrange on prepped baking sheets with 2-in. apart. Flatten balls to 1/4-in. thick.

3. In the preheated oven, bake about 8-10 minutes, until browned slightly.

Nutrition Information

Calories: 113 calories; Total Carbohydrate: 15.5g Cholesterol: 12 mg Total Fat: 5g Proteinr: 1.5g Sodium: 101 mg

BASIC SUGAR COOKIES

Serving: 18 - **Prep:** 15m - **Ready in:** 45m

INGREDIENTS

- 1/2 cup butter
- 2 cups Basic Cookie Mix
- 1 egg
- 1 tsp. vanilla extract

DIRECTION

1. Liquify butter on low heat and put into 2 cups Basic Cookie Mix.
2. Whip the egggently and put into the mixture. Mix vanilla in and combine thoroughly.
3. Form into an-inch balls using slightly floured hands and place on an oiled cookie sheet, spacing approximately 2-inch away.
4. Bake about 12 to 15 minutes at 180 ° C or 350 ° F tillgolden in color.
5. Allow a few minutes to cool then transfer from cookie sheet onto racks to cool fully.

Nutrition Information

Calories: 119 calories; Total Carbohydrate: 16g Cholesterol: 24 mg Total Fat: 5.4g Proteinr: 1.7g Sodium: 120 mg

BASIC SUGAR COOKIES - TRIED AND TRUE SINCE 1960

Serving: 48 - **Prep:** 30m - **Ready in:** 2h45m

INGREDIENTS

- 3 cups self-rising flour
- 1 cup butter at room temperature
- 1 cup white sugar, or more to taste
- 2 eggs at room temperature
- 1 1/2 tsps. vanilla extract
- 1/4 tsp. salt

DIRECTION

1. In a bowl, mix thoroughly the sugar, salt, vanilla extract, butter, self-rising flour, and eggs. Whisk the mixture for at least 5 minutes. Store the dough inside the refrigerator for at least 2 hours to overnight.
2. Set the oven to 275°F (135°C) for preheating.
3. Using a lightly floured rolling pin, roll the dough out onto a floured work surface. Use cutters to cut out cookies. Arrange the cookies into the baking sheets.
4. Let it bake inside the preheated oven for about 15 minutes until the bottoms of the cookies are lightlygolden brown.

Nutrition Information

Calories: 81 calories; Total Carbohydrate: 10g Cholesterol: 18 mg Total Fat: 4.1g Proteinr: 1.1g Sodium: 141 mg

SUGARY SUGAR COOKIES

Serving: 24

INGREDIENTS

- 1 cup white sugar
- 1 cup butter
- 2 eggs
- 3 1/2 cups sifted all-purpose flour
- 2 tsps. baking powder
- 2 tsps. vanilla extract

DIRECTION

1. Melt margarine or butter on low heat.
2. Combine eggs, butter and sugar together then beat well. Sift in baking powder and flour, then stir in vanilla. Drop dough on cookie sheets by tsp..
3. Bake at 190°C or 375°F until turngolden brown, about 10 to 15 minutes.

Nutrition Information

Calories: 174 calories; Total Carbohydrate: 22.4g Cholesterol: 36 mg Total Fat: 8.3g Proteinr: 2.5g Sodium: 101 mg

BETTY'S SUGAR COOKIES

Serving: 48 - **Prep:** 15m - **Ready in:** 45m

INGREDIENTS

- 1 cup shortening
- 1/2 cup white sugar
- 1/2 cup brown sugar
- 2 eggs
- 1 1/2 tsps. vanilla extrac t
- 2 1/4 cups all-purpose flour
- 1/2 tsp. baking soda
- 1/2 tsp. salt
- 1/4 cup colored sugar for decoration

DIRECTION

1. Heat the oven to 175 ° C or 350 ° F. Oil cookie sheets.
2. Cream white sugar, brown sugar and shortening in a big bowl till smooth. Whip in eggs, one by one then mix in vanilla. Mix baking soda, salt and flour; mix to creamed mixture. Form dough into balls of 1/2-inch and arrange them an-inch away on prepped cookie sheets. Press every ball a bit into flatten and scatter colored sugar over.
3. Bake in prepped oven, about 8 to 10 minutes. Cool cookies for 5 minutes on baking sheet then transfer onto wire rack and fully cool.

Nutrition Information

Calories: 80 calories; Total Carbohydrate: 9.1g Cholesterol: 8 mg Total Fat: 4.5g Proteinr: 0.9g Sodium: 41 mg

BETZ'SGOOD SUGAR COOKIES

Serving: 48 - **Prep:** 20m - **Ready in:** 9h

INGREDIENTS

- 1 cup butter
- 1 1/2 cups white sugar

- 2 eggs
- 1 tsp. vanilla extract
- 1 tsp. lemon extract
- 2 cups all-purpose flour
- 1 tsp. baking powder
- 1 pinch salt

DIRECTION

1. Cream sugar and butter together in a big bowl until fluffy. Whisk in the eggs, 1 egg each time, and then mix in lemon extracts and vanilla extracts. Mix salt, baking powder, and flour together; slowly mix into the creamed mixture to make a soft dough. Wrap or cover the dough, and chill overnight.
2. Start preheating the oven to 400°F (200°C). On a surface scattered with flour, roll the dough into 1/4 inch thick. Use a cookie cutter to cut into the wanted shapes. Put the cookies on non-oiled cookie sheets 2" apart.
3. Put in the preheated oven and bake until turning light brown, about 10 minutes. Put on wire racks to cool.

Nutrition Information

Calories: 81 calories; Total Carbohydrate: 10.3g Cholesterol: 18 mg Total Fat: 4.1g Proteinr: 0.8g Sodium: 40 mg

BIG SOFT SUGAR COOKIE CAKES

Serving: 18 - **Prep:** 10m - **Ready in:** 25m

INGREDIENTS

- 1 cup margarine
- 2 cups white sugar
- 2 eggs
- 1 cup milk
- 5 cups all-purpose flour
- 2 tsps. baking powder
- 1 tsp. baking soda
- 1 (16 oz.) can vanilla ready to spread frosting
- colored candy sprinkles

DIRECTION

1. Heat an oven to 190 ° C or 375 ° F.

2. Cream sugar and margarine together in a big bowl till smooth. Whip in eggs one by one, whipping thoroughly after each addition. Mix baking powder, baking soda and flour; mix into sugar mixture alternating with milk. Drop on unoiled cookie sheets by heaping tablespoonfuls. Place cookies not less than 3-inch away.

3. Bake in prepped oven, about 12 to 15 minutes, or till pale brown. Transfer from cookie sheets onto wire racks to let cool. Once fully cool, ice using vanilla icing and scatter candy sprinkles over.

Nutrition Information

Calories: 420 calories; Total Carbohydrate: 66.5g Cholesterol: 22 mg Total Fat: 15.2g Proteinr: 4.8g Sodium: 287 mg

BISCOCHITOS TRADITIONAL COOKIES

Serving: 72 - **Prep:** 15m - **Ready in:** 25m

INGREDIENTS

- 6 cups all-purpose flour
- 1 tbsp. baking powder
- 1/4 tsp. salt
- 2 cups lard
- 1 1/2 cups white sugar
- 2 tsps. anise seed
- 2 eggs
- 1/4 cup brandy
- 1/4 cup white sugar
- 1 tbsp.ground cinnamon

DIRECTION

1. Start preheating oven to 350°F (175°C). Sift salt, baking powder and flour into a bowl. Put aside.

2. Cream 1 1/2 cups of sugar and lard together in a large bowl until they become smooth. Mix in anise seed, then beat until they become fluffy. Then stir in eggs, 1 egg at a time. Put in brandy and sifted ingredients, stir until blended well.

3. Roll dough out on a floured surface to 1/2 or 1/4-in. thick, then cut with cookie cutters into the preferred

shapes. The traditional is fleur-de-lis. Arrange cookies on the baking sheets. Mix cinnamon and a quarter cup of sugar together; sprinkle over cookies tops.

4. Bake in prepared oven for 10 mins or until lightly browned at the bottoms.

Nutrition Information

Calories: 113 calories; Total Carbohydrate: 13g Cholesterol: 11 mg Total Fat: 5.9g Proteinr: 1.3g Sodium: 24 mg

BLUE RIBBON SUGAR COOKIES

Serving: 48 - **Prep:** 35m - **Ready in:** 1h

INGREDIENTS

- 3/4 cup butter, softened
- 1 cup vegetable oil
- 1 cup confectioners' sugar
- 1 cup white sugar
- 2 eggs
- 1 tsp. vanilla extract
- 1 1/2 tsps. lemon extract
- 4 cups all-purpose flour
- 1 tsp. cream of tarta r
- 1 tsp. baking soda
- 1 tsp. salt
- 1/2 cup white sugar for decoration

DIRECTION

1. Start preheating the oven to 375°F (190 °C). Sift together salt, baking soda, cream of tartar, and flour. Put aside.
2. Cream white sugar, confectioners' sugar, oil, and butter together in a big bowl until well mixed. Mix in lemon extracts, vanilla extracts, and eggs. Slowly stir in the dry ingredients until well mixed. Shape the dough into balls about the size of a walnut. Put the cookies on the baking sheet 2" part. Use a sugar-dipped bottom of aglass to flatten the cookies to 1/8 inch thickness. If you don't want to frost the cookies later, you can use colored sugar.
3. Put in the preheated oven and bake until the edges turngolden brown, about 9-12 minutes. Let the cookies stay in the baking sheet to cool for 5 minutes, and then transfer to a wire rack to fully cool.

Nutrition Information

Calories: 141 calories; Total Carbohydrate: 16.8g Cholesterol: 15 mg Total Fat: 7.7g Proteinr: 1.4g Sodium: 98 mg

BROWN RIM COOKIES

Serving: 60 - **Prep:** 10m - **Ready in:** 20m

INGREDIENTS

- 2 cups butter flavored shortening
- 1 1/3 cups white sugar
- 4 eggs
- 2 tsps. vanilla extract
- 5 cups all-purpose flour
- 2 tsps. salt

DIRECTION

1. Heat an oven to 190 ° C or 375 ° F. Oil cookie sheets.
2. Cream sugar and shortening in a big bowl. Whip in eggs, one by one, then mix vanilla in. Mix salt and flour; mix into creamed mixture to blend thoroughly. Drop on prepped cookie sheets by heaping spoonfuls.
3. Bake in the prepped oven, about 8 to 10 minutes. Once cookies are cool, flip over and check the underside to see the "brown rim".

Nutrition Information

Calories: 123 calories; Total Carbohydrate: 12.4g Cholesterol: 12 mg Total Fat: 7.6g Proteinr: 1.5g Sodium: 82 mg

BROWN SUGAR COOKIES I

Serving: 24

INGREDIENTS

- 2 cups all-purpose flour
- 1 1/2 tsps. baking powder

- 1 pinch salt
- 1/2 cup butter, softened
- 1 egg
- 1 tbsp. heavy whipping cream
- 1 1/2 tsps. vanilla extract
- 1/2 cup packed brown sugar

DIRECTION

1. Whisk together brown sugar and butter in a large mixing bowl. Beat in vanilla, heavy cream, and egg.
2. Gradually put in salt, baking powder, and flour. Mix until incorporated. If dough looks too dry, pour in water, 1/2 tsp. at a time .
3. Chill dough, covered, for 4 hours.
4. Set oven to 375°F to preheat.
5. On a work surface coated with flour, roll dough out to a 1/8-inch thick. Cut out shapes using cookie cutters and arrange 1 1/2 inches apart on cookie sheets.
6. Bake cookies in the preheated oven until lightly colored, for 8 to 10 minutes.

Nutrition Information

Calories: 95 calories; Total Carbohydrate: 12.6g Cholesterol: 19 mg Total Fat: 4.4g Proteinr: 1.4g Sodium: 69 mg

BROWN SUGAR COOKIES II

Serving: 30

INGREDIENTS

- 2/3 cup shortening
- 2/3 cup butter, softened
- 1 cup white sugar
- 1 cup packed brown sugar
- 2 eggs
- 2 tsps. vanilla extract
- 3 1/4 cups all-purpose flour
- 1 tsp. baking soda
- 1 tsp. salt

DIRECTION

1. Mix vanilla, eggs, sugars, margarine or butter and shortening thoroughly. Mix in unbleached or all-purpose flour, salt and baking soda.
2. Turn the dough onto the lightly floured board. Using lightly floured hands, form the dough into ball, pressing to create the dough compact. Divide the dough in half.
3. On floured board, roll each doughgently back and forth to form each 1/2 into roll 2-inch in diameter, about 8-inch long. Roll the dough onto the plastic wrap: encase and tightly twist ends. The dough can be frozen up to 3 months or refrigerate up to 1 month.
4. Start preheating the oven to 375 °F (190°C).
5. Slice roll into 1/4 inches pieces. (It isn't necessary to thaw the frozen dough before cutting.) On unoiled baking sheet, arrange slices 2-inch apart. Bake for 9-11 minutes. Transfer cookies immediately from the baking sheet onto the wire rack.
6. CHOCOLATE CHIP: Put in one cup of the chopped nuts and one cup of the mini semisweet chocolate chips with flour. OATMEAL-COCONUT: Reduce the flour to 2 3/4 cups. Put in one cup of the quick-cooking oats and one cup of the flaked coconut with flour. PEANUT BUTTER: Put in one cup of the chunky or creamy peanut butter with shortening. CHOCOLATE-NUT: Put in half cup of cocoa and one cup of the chopped nuts with flour. FRUIT SLICES: Put in half cup of cut-up mixed candied fruit, one cup of the whole candied cherries and half cup of the chopped nuts with flour.

Nutrition Information

Calories: 185 calories; Total Carbohydrate: 24.3g Cholesterol: 23 mg Total Fat: 9.1g Proteinr: 1.9g Sodium: 156 mg

BROWN SUGAR DROPS

Serving: 72 **- Prep:** 10m **- Ready in:** 1h30m

INGREDIENTS

- 1 cup shortening
- 2 cups packed brown sugar
- 2 eggs
- 1/2 cup buttermil k
- 3 1/2 cups all-purpose flour
- 1 tsp. baking soda
- 1 tsp. salt

DIRECTION

1. Cream brown sugar and shortening together in a big bowl until smooth. Beat in 1 egg at a time and stir in buttermilk. Mix together salt, baking soda and flour, then stir into the buttermilk mixture until well-combined. Cover the dough and refrigerate for a minimum of 1 hour.
2. Set the oven to 200°C or 400°F to preheat. Coat cookie sheets withgrease. Drop on prepared cookie sheets with rounded teaspoonfuls of dough, 2 inches apart.
3. In the preheated oven, bake until nearly no imprint left when touching with your finger, about 8-10 minutes. Take out of the cookie sheets instantly to cool on wire racks.

Nutrition Information

Calories: 73 calories; Total Carbohydrate: 10.7g Cholesterol: 5 mg Total Fat: 3.1g Proteinr: 0.9g Sodium: 55 mg

BUNNY COOKIES

Serving: 48

INGREDIENTS

- 1 1/4 cups white sugar
- 2/3 cup shortening
- 2 eggs
- 3 1/2 cups all-purpose flour
- 1/2 tsp. salt
- 2 tsps. baking powder
- 2 1/2 tsps. orange zest
- 1 tbsp. orange juice
- 1/4 cup cinnamon red hot candies

DIRECTION

1. Turn oven to 375°F (190°C) to preheat.
2. Whisk together shortening and sugar in a large bowl. Whisk in eggs until incorporated. Mix in baking powder, salt, and flour until well combined. Stir in orange zest and orange juice.
3. Flatten dough to a thickness of 1/4 inch on a work surface lightly coated with flour. Cut out rabbit shapes using a cookie cutter. Arrange rabbits onto a cookie sheet; position a cinnamon candies onto the rabbits for eyes. Bake cookies in the heated oven for 8 to 10 minutes. Add frosting if desired.

Nutrition Information

Calories: 86 calories; Total Carbohydrate: 13.4g Cholesterol: 8 mg Total Fat: 3.1g Proteinr: 1.2g Sodium: 48 mg

BUTTERMILK COOKIES

Serving: 36 - **Prep:** 20m - **Ready in:** 26m

INGREDIENTS

- 1 cup shortening
- 2 cups white sugar
- 4 eggs
- 4 cups all-purpose flour
- 4 tsps. baking powder
- 2 tsps. baking soda
- 1 tsp. salt
- 1 cup buttermilk
- 4 tsps. vanilla extract

DIRECTION

1. Preheat an oven to 220 °C or 425 °F. Oil cookie sheets.
2. Cream together the sugar and shortening in a big bowl. Whisk in eggs, one by one, then mix in vanilla. Into the creamed mixture, mix the salt, baking soda, baking powder and flour, mix alternately with buttermilk. Onto the prepped cookie sheets, drop by rounded spoonfuls.
3. In the prepped oven, allow to bake for 6 to 8 minutes. On baking sheet, let the cookies cool for 5 minutes prior to taking to a wire rack to cool fully.

Nutrition Information

Calories: 157 calories; Total Carbohydrate: 22.3g Cholesterol: 24 mg Total Fat: 6.4g Proteinr: 2.4g Sodium: 204 mg

CHAI BUTTER COOKIES

Serving: 36 - **Prep:** 15m - **Ready in:** 27m

INGREDIENTS

- 1 cup unsalted butter
- 1 cup chai tea mix
- 1 1/3 cups white sugar
- 2 eggs
- 3 1/2 cups all-purpose flour
- 1 tbsp. baking powder
- 2 tsps. salt
- 1/2 cup white sugar for decoration

DIRECTION

1. Whisk together chai tea mix, 1 1/3 cups sugar, and butter in a large mixing bowl until fluffy and light. Beat in eggs, one by one, beating well between additions. Mix salt, baking powder, and flour together; mix into creamed mixture just until moistened. Refrigerate dough, covered, for 1 hour.
2. Set oven to 400°F (200°C) to preheat. Form cookie dough into walnut-sized balls, then roll in sugar to coat. Arrange cookies 3 inches apart ongreased cookie sheets; slightly press cookies using the tines of a fork.
3. Bake cookies in the preheated oven for 10 to 12 minutes or until edges start browning. Transfer cookies from the cookie sheets to wire racks to cool.

Nutrition Information
Calories: 141 calories; Total Carbohydrate: 21g Cholesterol: 24 mg Total Fat: 5.7g Proteinr: 1.8g Sodium: 164 mg

PUMPKIN SPICE SNICKERDOODLES

Serving: 18 - **Prep:** 15m - **Ready in:** 30m

INGREDIENTS

- 1 1/2 cups all-purpose flour
- 1/2 tsp. kosher salt
- 1/2 tsp. baking soda
- 1/4 tsp. cream of tartar
- 1/2 tsp.ground cinnamon
- 1/2 tsp.ginger

- 1/4 tsp. allspice
- 1/4 tsp. ground cloves
- 1/8 tsp. nutmeg
- 1/2 cup unsalted butter
- 1/2 cup white sugar
- 1/3 cup light brown sugar, packed
- 1 tsp. vanilla extract
- 1 large egg

Rolling Sugar:

- 1/4 cup white sugar
- 2 tsps. cinnamon

Glaze (Optional):

- 1/4 cup confectioners' sugar
- 1 tbsp. milk, or as needed

DIRECTION

1. Preheat an oven to 175 °C or 350 °F. Line a parchment paper or silicone mat on a rimmed baking sheet.
2. In a mixing bowl, put cream of tartar, baking soda, salt and flour. Put in nutmeg, clove, allspice, ginger and cinnamon. Mix for 1 or 2 minutes till well blended.
3. In another mixing bowl, put brown sugar, sugar and butter. Using a wooden spoon or spatula, cream together for 2 or 3 minutes till mixture is smooth. Put in egg and vanilla. Mix till well incorporated.
4. Into the butter mixture, transfer the flour mixture. Mix till just blended or till flour disappears.
5. With plastic wrap, wrap the bowl. Refrigerate dough to chill for approximately an hour.
6. In a plate or shallow bowl, mix together the sugar and cinnamon.
7. Spoon dough to make 2 tbsp. balls. Coat every side by rolling in cinnamon-sugar mixture. Roll into smooth ball and put on prepped baking sheet about 3- to 4-inch apart. Slightly flatten.
8. In prepped oven, bake for 10 to 12 minutes till browned.
9. Let cool for 5 minutes on a baking sheet; scatter more cinnamon-sugar mixture on top, if wished. Onto cooling rack, turn out the cookies to cool completely.
10. Brush cookies with a simpleglaze to add a bit of a shine, if desired. To attain brushing consistency, mix confectioners' sugar with lemon juice or milk. Brush on cookies. Scatter pumpkin pie spice or additional cinnamon sugar on top, if wished.

Nutrition Information

Calories: 144 calories; Total Carbohydrate: 22.4g Cholesterol: 24 mg Total Fat: 5.5g Proteinr: 1.5g
Sodium: 95 mg

CHEWY SUGAR COOKIES

Serving: 30 - **Prep:** 10m - **Ready in:** 25m

INGREDIENTS

- 2 3/4 cups all-purpose flour
- 1 tsp. baking soda
- 1/2 tsp. salt
- 1 1/4 cups margarine
- 2 cups white sugar
- 2 eggs
- 2 tsps. vanilla extract
- 1/4 cup white sugar for decoration

DIRECTION

1. Set an oven to 175°C (350°F) to preheat. Stir together the salt, baking soda and flour in a medium bowl, then put aside.
2. Cream together the 2 cups of sugar and margarine in a big bowl, until becoming fluffy and light. Beat in the eggs, one by one, followed by the vanilla. Slowly stir in the dry ingredients until just combined. Roll the dough into walnut-sized balls, then roll the balls in the leftover 1/4 cup of sugar. Put the cookies onto the ungreased cookie sheets, placing 2 inches apart; flatten a bit.
3. Bake in the preheated oven for 8-10 minutes, until the edges turn a bit brown. Let the cookies cool for 5 minutes on the baking tray prior to transferring to a wire rack to fully cool .

Nutrition Information

Calories: 172 calories; Total Carbohydrate: 23.9g Cholesterol: 12 mg Total Fat: 7.9g Proteinr: 1.7g Sodium: 173 mg

CHOCOLATE AND VANILLA SUGAR COOKIES

Serving: 36 - **Prep:** 27m - **Ready in:** 1h35m

INGREDIENTS

- 3 (1 oz.) squares semisweet chocolate
- 1 cup unsalted butter, softened
- 1 cup SPLENDA Sugar Blend
- 2 large eggs
- 2 tsps. vanilla extract
- 4 cups all-purpose flour
- 1 tsp. baking powder
- 1/4 tsp. salt

DIRECTION

1. In a large mixing bowl, whisk butter using an electric mixer at medium speed until creamy. Slowly beat in Splenda sugar blend until well distributed. Beat in eggs, one by one, mixing well between additions. Whisk in vanilla.
2. In a microwave oven at high power, microwave chocolate in a 1-cupglass measuring cup for 60 to 90 seconds, stirring 2 times, until melted. Set to one side.
3. In a separate mixing bowl, mix salt, flour and baking powder. Slowly beat flour mixture into Splenda sugar blend mixture until combined without overmixing. Cut dough in half. Whisk melted chocolate in half of mixture.
4. Lay dough on a work surface lightly coated with flour.
5. To make checker board cookies, form chocolate dough into two 1-inch-diameter rectangular logs. Do the same with vanilla dough. Slice each log vertically into quarters.gather logs together again, alternating vanilla and chocolate to have a checkerboard pattern.
6. To make pinwheel cookies, flatten chocolate dough into two 8x9-inch rectangles. Flatten vanilla dough into two 8x10-inch rectangles. Lay the vanilla dough on bottom, making sure that it extends 1 inch beyond the chocolate dough; roll like jelly-roll.
7. To make striped cookies, separate each flavor into 3 balls. Shape each ball into a 7 1/2 x1/3-inch rectangle; slice each rectangle into five 1 1/2x3-inch strips. Stack 5 strips alternating vanilla and chocolate.
8. Use plastic wrap to wrap logs. Refrigerate until dough is briefly set, approximately 1 hour. (Dough at this point can be stored in the freezer for a maximum of 3 months).
9. Turn oven to 350°F to preheat. Lightly butter cookie sheets.
10. Take dough out of the fridge. Cut cookie dough into slices about 1/4 inch in thickness; arrange ongreased cookie sheets.
11. Bake cookies at 350°F until they are lightly browned, for 8 to 10 minutes. Allow to cool briefly on cookie sheets. Transfer cookies to wire racks and allow to cool thoroughly.

CHRISTMAS COOKIE CUT OUTS

Serving: 24 - **Prep:** 30m - **Ready in:** 10h40m

INGREDIENTS

- 3 cups all-purpose flour
- 2 tsps. cream of tartar
- 1 tsp. baking soda
- 1 tsp.ground nutmeg
- 1 pinchground cinnamon
- 1 cup butter, softened
- 1 cup white sugar
- 3 eggs, beaten
- 1 tsp. vanilla extract

Frosting:

- 4 cups confectioners' sugar
- 1/2 cup butter, softened
- 1 tbsp. vanilla extract
- 1/4 cup milk
- any color food coloring (optional)

DIRECTION

1. In a bowl, sift the cinnamon, nutmeg, baking soda, cream of tartar and flour together; put aside. Use an electric mixer to whip the sugar and butter till smooth in a big bowl. Put in eggs, one by one, blending each egg into mixture of butter prior to putting the next. Whip in vanilla including the final egg. Stir in flour mixture barely to incorporate. Chill dough with cover overnight.
2. Heat the oven to 175 ° C or 350 ° F. On floured counter, unroll dough to half-inch thickness. Use Christmas cookie cutters to cut out shapes. Arrange cookies on unprepped cookie sheets an-inch away.
3. Bake for 8 to 10 minutes in prepped oven till edges turngolden. Lower the baking time in case using cutters with small appendages, like reindeer legs, otherwise they will burn. Transfer cookies to wire rack and fully cool.
4. Use an electric mixer to whip confectioners' sugar and butter in a big bowl, mixture will become firm.

Put in vanilla andgradually stir in milk, a small amount at one time to attain a spreadable consistency. Mix food coloring in, if wished. Ensure cookies are fully cool to frost.

Nutrition Information

Calories: 282 calories; Total Carbohydrate: 40.7g Cholesterol: 54 mg Total Fat: 12.4g Proteinr: 2.6g Sodium: 145 mg

CINNAMON-SUGAR COOKIES

Serving: 72 **- Ready in:** 3h

INGREDIENTS

- 1½ cups white whole-wheat flour (see Tip)
- 1½ cups all-purpose flour
- 3 tsps.ground cinnamon, divided
- 1¼ tsps. baking powder
- ¼ tsp. baking soda
- ¼ tsp. salt
- 1 cup plus 1 tsp. sugar, divided
- 5 tbsps. canola oil
- 4 tbsps. unsalted butter, at room temperature
- 2 large eggs
- 2 tsps. vanilla extract

DIRECTION

1. In a medium bowl, whisk together salt, baking soda, baking powder, 2 tsps. of cinnamon, all-purpose flour, and white whole-wheat flour.
2. In a mixing bowl, use an electric mixer on high to beat butter, oil, and 1 cup of sugar together until smooth, scraping the sides of the bowl down. Add the vanilla and eggs, beat until smooth, scraping the sides down. Add the flour mixture and mix on a low speed just until combined .
3. Place 1/2 of the dough onto a big plastic wrap piece and shape into a log that's 10-inches long (it doesn't need to be perfectly round). Repeat with the other 1/2 dough. Wrap them and freeze until the logs are just firm, roughly 45 minutes. Re-roll the logs to make them even rounder and place back into the freezer until really firm, a minimum of 1 more hour.
4. Set the oven to 350 degrees Fahrenheit. Use a silicone mat or parchment paper to line a baking sheet.
5. Take one dough roll at a time out of the freezer and let sit at room temperature for about 5 minutes.

Unwrap and slice the dough into 1/4 inch-thick rounds crosswise, turning dough a quarter turn after each slice to keep cookies round. Place them onto the baking sheet, 1/2 inch apart. Shape the dough using fingers if the cookies are not round as desired. In a small bowl, combine leftover a tsp. each of sugar and cinnamon and sprinkle a bit onto each cookie.

6. Bake cookies for 8 minutes to make them soft or 10 minutes to make them crisp. Move to a wire rack to completely cool. Repeat with the remaining dough roll if you want.

Nutrition Information

Calories: 46 calories; Total Carbohydrate: 7g Cholesterol: 7 mg Total Fat: 2g Fiber: 0g Proteinr: 1g Sodium: 24 mg Sugar: 3g Saturated Fat: 1g

CITRUS-KISSED HONEY BUTTONS

Serving: 36 - **Ready in:** 1h15m

INGREDIENTS

- 1¾ cups all-purpose flour
- ½ tsp. baking soda
- ½ tsp. cream of tartar
- ¼ tsp. salt
- 1 cupgranulated sugar
- 4 tbsps. unsalted butter, softened (see Tip)
- 1 large egg
- 1 tbsp. honey
- 1 tbsp. finelygrated lemon zest
- 1 tbsp. finelygrated orange zest
- 1 tsp. lemon extract

DIRECTION

1. In a small bowl, combine salt, cream of tartar, baking soda and flour.
2. In a mixing bowl, use an electric mixer to beat together butter and sugar on medium-high speed until fluffy and light. Put in lemon extract, orange zest, lemon zest, honey and egg; beat until blended. Beat in the flour mixturegradually on low speed barely until mixed. Put the dough into the refrigerator with cover overnight or at least for 30 minutes.

3. Turn on the oven to 375 degrees F to preheat. Use nonstick baking mats or parchment paper to line 2 large baking sheets.
4. Use your hands to form 36 balls from the dough (approximately 2 level tsps. each). On prepped baking sheets, arrange balls 2 inches apart from each other.
5. Put into the oven to bake for 6-8 minutes, one batch at a time, until they start to crack and puffed. Allow the cool for 2 minutes on baking sheets, then remove them onto wire rack to cool fully.

Nutrition Information

Calories: 60 calories; Total Carbohydrate: 11 g Cholesterol: 9 mg Total Fat: 1g Fiber: 0g Proteinr: 1g Sodium: 36 mg Sugar: 6g Saturated Fat: 1g

COCONUT ROLLED SUGAR COOKIES

Serving: 42

INGREDIENTS

- 1 cup butter
- 1 cup white sugar
- 1 tbsp. milk
- 1 tsp. vanilla extract
- 2 1/2 cups all-purpose flour
- 1 cup finely chopped red andgreen candied cherries
- 1/2 cup chopped pecans
- 1 cup flaked coconut

DIRECTION

1. Beat margarine or butter in mixing bowl until softened. Put in sugar, then beat until fluffy. Put in vanilla and milk; mix well.
2. Put in flour, then beat until they are well mixed. Mix in pecans and cherries.
3. Form into 3 7-inch long rolls. Coat by rolling in coconut.
4. Cover with the plastic wrap. Let chill for several hours or overnight.
5. Start preheating the oven to 375°F.
6. Slice the rolls into 1/4-inch slices. Arrange onto an unoiled cookie sheet. Bake until done, about 12 mins. Bring over to the wire rack to cool.

Nutrition Information

Calories: 112 calories; Total Carbohydrate: 14.1g Cholesterol: 12 mg Total Fat: 5.9g Proteinr: 1g Sodium: 39 mg

COOKIE JAR SUGAR COOKIES

Serving: 12

INGREDIENTS

To Layer In Jar:
- 1 1/2 cups white sugar
- 4 cups all-purpose flour
- 1 tsp. baking powder
- 1/2 tsp. baking soda
- 1/2 tsp. salt
- 3/4 tsp.ground nutmeg

To Mix The Cookies:
- 1 cup butter, room temperature
- 1 egg
- 1/2 cup sour cream
- 1 tsp. vanilla extract

DIRECTION

1. Mix flour with nutmeg, baking soda, salt, and baking powder. Layer the white sugar followed by flour mixture in a clean 1-quartglass jar with a wide mouth. Pack firmly in place and seal. Attach a card following these directions:
2. Whisk 1 cup butter at room temperature in a large mixing bowl until fluffy and light. Whisk in 1 egg until incorporated. Add 1 tsp. vanilla and 1/2 cup of sour cream; beat at low speed. Slowly put in contents of jar; beat until thoroughly combined. Wrap cookies in foil or plastic wrap; chill for a couple of hours to overnight. Take dough out of the fridge. Turn oven to 375°F (190°C) to preheat. Flatten chilled dough on a work surface lightly coated with flour; cut out desired shapes. Lay cookies on an unbuttered cookie sheet. Bake cookies in the preheated oven until edges turngolden brown, for 10 to 12 minutes.

Nutrition Information
Calories: 412 calories; Total Carbohydrate: 57.5g Cholesterol: 59 mg Total Fat: 18.2g Proteinr: 5.2g Sodium: 310 mg

COOKIE MOLD SUGAR COOKIES

Serving: 48

INGREDIENTS

- 1 cup white sugar
- 3 cups all-purpose flour
- 1 cup butter, softened
- 1 tbsp. vanilla extract
- 2 eggs
- 1 tsp. salt

DIRECTION

1. Beat butter for 1 minute until creamy; put in sugar and beat for 3 more minutes. Beat eggs and vanilla into butter mixture, approximately 1 minute. Add salt and flour; beat for 1 minute, scraping down sides of the mixing bowl. Chill dough in the fridge for 1 to 2 hours.
2. Turn oven to 375°F (190°C) to preheat.
3. Grease a mold with cooking spray or vegetable oil. Coat mold with flour, tapping off excess. Pack dough into the prepared mold, using a knife to scrape off excess so that dough is flush with the mold's edge. Loosen edges and allow dough to fall onto an unbuttered cookie sheet.
4. Bake cookies in the preheated oven until they turn brown lightly, for 12 to 15 minutes. Allow cookies to cool for a couple of minutes before taking them out of the sheet.

Nutrition Information

Calories: 82 calories; Total Carbohydrate: 10.2g Cholesterol: 18 mg Total Fat: 4.1g Proteinr: 1.1g Sodium: 79 mg

CRACKED SUGAR COOKIES I

Serving: 36 - Prep: 20m - Ready in: 35m

INGREDIENTS

- 2 cups white sugar
- 1/2 cup butter, softened
- 1/2 cup vegetable oil

- 3 egg yolks
- 2 cups all-purpose flour
- 1 tsp. baking soda
- 1 tsp. cream of tartar
- 1 pinch salt
- 1/2 tsp. vanilla extract
- 1/4 cup white sugar, for rolling

DIRECTION

1. Heat an oven to 150 °C or 300 °F.
2. Use an electric mixer to whip butter, vegetable oil and 2 cups sugar in big bowl till smooth. Put in the egg yolks, one by one, letting every egg to mix into butter mixture prior to putting the next. In mixture of egg yolk, sift salt, cream of tartar, baking soda and flour; mix. Mix vanilla extract in. Form dough into balls with the size of walnut.
3. Smear quarter cup of sugar on an even surface. Roll dough balls in sugar to cover. Place on baking sheets, spacing no less than 2 inches away.
4. Bake in prepped oven for 15 minutes till cooked in the center, yet not brown .

Nutrition Information

Calories: 128 calories; Total Carbohydrate: 17.9g Cholesterol: 24 mg Total Fat: 6g Proteinr: 1g Sodium: 54 mg

CRACKED SUGAR COOKIES II

Serving: 24

INGREDIENTS

- 1 1/4 cups white sugar
- 1 cup butter
- 3 egg yolks
- 1 tsp. vanilla extract
- 2 1/2 cups all-purpose flour
- 1 tsp. baking soda
- 1/2 tsp. cream of tartar

DIRECTION

1. Set oven to 350°F (180°C) to preheat. Lightly oil 2 cookie sheets.

2. Whisk together butter and sugar. Whisk in vanilla and egg yolks.

3. Stir in cream of tartar, baking soda, and flour.

4. Shape dough into walnut-sized balls; lay the balls on thegreased cookie sheets, placing them 2 inches apart. Do not press dough down. Bake cookies in the preheated oven until tops are cracked and colored, approximately 10 to 11 minutes.

Nutrition Information

Calories: 163 calories; Total Carbohydrate: 20.5g Cholesterol: 46 mg Total Fat: 8.4g Proteinr: 1.8g Sodium: 108 mg

CRACKED SUGAR COOKIES III

Serving: 66 - **Prep:** 1day1h15m - **Ready in:** 1day1h23m

INGREDIENTS

- 1 cup shortening
- 1 1/2 cups white sugar
- 2 eggs
- 2 tsps. vanilla extract
- 2 1/2 cups all-purpose flour
- 2 tsps. baking powder
- 1/2 tsp. salt
- 1/4 cup white sugar for decoration

DIRECTION

1. Whisk together 1 1/2 cups sugar and shortening in a large mixing bowl until no lumps remain. Whisk in eggs, one by one; stir in vanilla. Mix baking powder, salt, and flour together; whisk into creamed mixture until well distributed. Chill, covered, for a minimum of 1 hour.

2. Turn oven to 350°F (175°C) to preheat. Shape dough into balls approximately 1 inch in diameter; roll in the rest of sugar to coat. Lay cookies on ungreased cookie sheets; separate cookies 2 inches apart.

3. Bake cookies at 350°F (175°C) until they are justgolden, for 8 to 9 minutes. Let cookies cool for 2 minutes on baking sheet, then bringing them to wire racks to cool entirely.

Nutrition Information

Calories: 68 calories; Total Carbohydrate: 9g Cholesterol: 6 mg Total Fat: 3.3g Proteinr: 0.7g Sodium: 31 mg

CRACKLED SUGAR COOKIES IV

Serving: 48 - **Prep:** 35m - **Ready in:** 50m

INGREDIENTS

- ½ cup butter, softened
- ½ cup shortening
- 2 cups sugar (see Tips)
- 1 tsp. baking soda
- 1 tsp. cream of tartar
- ⅛ tsp. salt
- 3 egg yolks
- ½ tsp. vanilla
- 1¾ cups all-purpose flour

DIRECTION

1. Heat an oven to 300°F. Whip shortening and butter in a big mixing bowl on moderate to high speed of an electric mixer for half a minute. Put in the salt, cream of tartar, baking soda and sugar. Whip the mixture to combine, scrape the bowl sides from time to time as you do. Whip in vanilla and egg yolks. Whip in as much of flour as possible using mixer. Mix in any leftover flour.
2. Form the dough balls about 1-inch in size. Arrange the balls on unprepped cookie sheets, 2-inch away.
3. Bake till edges are firm, about 12 to 14 minutes; prevent edges from browning. Let cookies cool on cookie sheet for 2 minutes. Remove cookies onto wire racks and cool.

Nutrition Information

Calories: 90 calories; Total Carbohydrate: 12g Cholesterol: 19 mg Total Fat: 4g Fiber: 0g Proteinr: 1g Sodium: 41 mg Sugar: 8g Saturated Fat: 2g

CRANBERRY-PISTACHIO SUGAR COOKIE THINS

Serving: 48 - **Ready in:** 2h45m

INGREDIENTS

- 2 cups all-purpose flour
- ⅔ cup white whole-wheat flour (see Tip)
- 1½ tsps. baking powder
- ¼ tsp. salt
- ⅓ cup canola oil or corn oil
- 4 tbsps. unsalted butter, slightly softened
- 1 cup plus 1 tbsp.granulated sugar, plus ½ cup, divided
- 1 large egg
- Finelygrated zest of 1 medium lemon
- ¼ cup plus 1 tbsp. honey
- 2½ tsps. vanilla extract
- ½ tsp. almond extract or lemon extract
- ¼ cup chopped pistachios
- ¼ cup chopped dried cranberries

DIRECTION

1. In the middle of the oven, place a rack; turn on the oven to 350 degrees F to preheat. Use parchment paper to line a large baking sheet(s).
2. In a large bowl, combine salt, baking powder, whole-wheat flour and all-purpose flour. In a large mixing bowl, use an electric mixer to beat together lemon zest, egg, 1/2 cup plus 1 tbsp. sugar, butter and oil on low speed until well-blended and smooth. Whip in lemon (or almond) extract, vanilla and honey until well-incorporated.
3. Beat approximately 1/2 of the floured mixture into the wet ingredients using mixer on low speed then medium speed until mixed. Whip the rest of flour mixture until just blended.
4. Split the dough into 4 pieces. Form a "log" of 9-inch length from each piece. Cut the log into 12 even pieces. Form a ball from each piece. On the prepped baking sheet, arrange the balls and put into the refrigerator for about 1 hour until very cold.
5. On a small plate, add the remaining 1/2 cup ofgranulated sugar. Dip the top of each dough ball into the sugar one at a time; arrange on another baking sheet 2 1/2 inch apart, sugar side up. Use cooking spray

to coat the bottom of a wideglass; dip into the sugar. Use theglass to flatten the balls to form 2 1/4-inch diameter cookies. Dip theglass into the sugar between cookies and coat with cooking spray if necessary.

6. Use cranberries and pistachios to sprinkle onto cookies; pat softly to help them stick.

7. Put the 1 pan of cookies at a time into the center rack to bake for 8-13 minutes until just firm to the touch. Allow to stand for 5 minutes; remove to wire racks and cool.

Nutrition Information

Calories: 79 calories; Total Carbohydrate: 12g Cholesterol: 6 mg Total Fat: 3g Fiber: 0g Proteinr: 1g Sodium: 29 mg Sugar: 7g Saturated Fat: 1g

CREAM CHEESE CUT-OUTS II

Serving: 48 **- Prep:** 30m **- Ready in:** 38m

INGREDIENTS

- 1/2 cup butter, softened
- 1 (3 oz.) package cream cheese
- 1 cup white sugar
- 1 egg
- 1/2 tsp. vanilla extract
- 2 cups all-purpose flour
- 1/2 tsp. baking powder

DIRECTION

1. In the big bowl, cream sugar, cream cheese and butter together till fluffy and light. Whip in vanilla and egg. Mix baking powder and flour; whisk into creamed mixture. Split the dough into two pieces, covered and chilled for roughly 60 minutes or till firm.

2. Preheat oven to 190 degrees C (375 degrees F). Onto the lightly floured surface, roll the dough out into 1/8-in. thickness. Chop into the shapes that you like with the cookie cutters and arrange cookies no less than 1 in. apart on the ungreased cookie sheets.

3. Bake in preheated oven till the cookies become firm and the bottom becomes a bit brown or for 7 - 9 minutes. Take out of the cookie sheets to cool down on the wire racks.

Nutrition Information

Calories: 60 calories; Total Carbohydrate: 8.2g Cholesterol: 11 mg Total Fat: 2.7g Proteinr: 0.8g Sodium: 24 mg

CREAMY LEMON SUGAR COOKIES

Serving: 12 - **Prep:** 15m - **Ready in:** 52m

INGREDIENTS

- 3 tbsps. white sugar
- 1 tbsp. lemon juice
- 3/4 cup white sugar
- 1/2 cup butter, softened
- 2 egg yolks
- 2 tsps. lemon juice
- 1 tsp. vanilla extract
- 1 1/4 cups all-purpose flour
- 1/2 tsp. half-and-half
- 1/2 tsp. baking soda

DIRECTION

1. Set the oven to 175°C or 350°F to preheat. Coat 2 baking sheets lightly withgrease.
2. In a small bowl, mix together 1 tbsp. of lemon juice and 3 tbsp. of white sugar.
3. In a big bowl, use an electric mixer to beat butter and sugar together. Beat vanilla extract, 2 tsp. of lemon juice and egg yolks into butter mixture. Put in baking soda, half-and-half and flour, then stir until dough is just blended.
4. Roll dough into balls the size of a walnut and coat each ball in the lemon sugar mixture, allowing excess to drip off. Arrange onto prepped baking sheets, 2 in. apart.
5. In the preheated oven, bake for 12-15 minutes, until edges turngolden. Allow to cool on baking sheet for 5 minutes prior to moving to a wire rack to cool thoroughly, about 20 minutes longer.

Nutrition Information

Calories: 186 calories; Total Carbohydrate: 25.9g Cholesterol: 55 mg Total Fat: 8.6g Proteinr: 1.9g Sodium: 109 mg

SUGAR COOKIES

Serving: 24 - **Prep:** 35m - **Ready in:** 1h15m

INGREDIENTS

- 1 cup shortening
- 2 cups white sugar
- 4 eggs
- 1 tsp. vanilla extract
- 4 cups all-purpose flour
- 2 tsps. baking powder
- 1 tsp. baking soda
- 1 cup buttermilk
- 1/2 cup butter, melted
- 2 cups confectioners' sugar
- 2 tbsps. milk
- 3 drops red food coloring (optional)

DIRECTION

1. Preheat the oven to 175 degrees C (350 degrees F). Line parchment paper onto cookie sheets.
2. Cream together the white sugar and shortening in a large bowl until the mix is smooth. Beat in the eggs one by one and then mix in vanilla. Mix the flour, baking soda and baking powder. Mix into creamed mixture alternating with buttermilk until youget a soft dough. Transfer onto the prepared cookie sheets, dropping by teaspoonfuls.
3. Bake in the preheated oven for about 10 minutes or until turned light brown. Let to cool on wire racks.
4. Blend together confectioners' sugar and melted butter in a medium bowl until smooth. Slowly mix in the milk until the frosting reaches the consistency desired. If desired, stir in food coloring. Pour over the cooled cookies and then transfer the frosted cookies onto cooling racks or waxed paper until the frosting is set.

Nutrition Information

Calories: 306 calories; Total Carbohydrate: 43.3g Cholesterol: 42 mg Total Fat: 13.6g Proteinr: 3.6g Sodium: 144 mg

DEAD BONES (L'OSSA MORTE)

Serving: 30 - **Prep:** 20m - **Ready in:** 12h35m

INGREDIENTS

- 1 lb. confectioners' sugar
- 2 1/2 cups all-purpose flour
- 2 1/2 tsps. baking powder
- 2 1/2 tsps.ground cloves
- 3 eggs, lightly beaten

DIRECTION

1. Mix together cloves, baking powder, flour, and sugar. Form a well in the sugar mixture; put eggs into the well. Use a fork to mix eggs into the mixture, then use your hands to mix, till the mixture becomes a smooth dough.
2. Line foil on a baking tray. Form dough into 1-in. balls; arrange on the prepared baking tray, spacing 2 inches apart. Use the bottom of aglass to flatten each cookie. Use a clean dish towel to cover the cookies; allow to rest all night. The cookies will spread.
3. Set oven to 175° C (350° F) and start preheating.
4. Place in the preheated oven and bake 15 minutes untilgolden. Take cookies out of pan right after the moment they are taken out of the oven (to avoid sticking). Place on a wire rack to cool completely.

Nutrition Information

Calories: 105 calories; Total Carbohydrate: 23.3g Cholesterol: 19 mg Total Fat: 0.6g Proteinr: 1.7g Sodium: 48 mg

FROSTED CUT-OUT SUGAR COOKIES

Serving: 36 - **Prep:** 10m - **Ready in:** 18m

INGREDIENTS

- 3/4 cup butter flavored shortening
- 1 cup white sugar
- 2 eggs
- 1 tbsp. milk
- 1 tsp. vanilla extract
- 2 1/2 cups all-purpose flour
- 1 tsp. baking powder
- 1 tsp. salt
- 1 tbsp. butter

- 1 tsp. vanilla extract
- 2 1/2 cups confectioners' sugar
- 3 tbsps. milk
- 2 drops any color food coloring

DIRECTION

1. Beat together white sugar and shortening in a large mixing bowl until no lumps remain. Beat in eggs, one by one; whisk in 1 tsp. vanilla and milk. Mix salt, baking powder, and flour together; beat into creamed mixture. Refrigerate dough, covered, for a minimum of 60 minutes.
2. Turn oven to 400°F (200°C) to preheat. Lightly oil cookie sheets, or line with parchment paper; Flatten dough to a thickness of 1/4 inch on a work surface lightly coated with flour. Cut out desired shapes using cookie cutters. Arrange cookies on prepared cookie sheets, placing them 1 1/2 inches apart.
3. Bake cookies in the preheated oven for 6 to 8 minutes. Transfer cookies from the baking sheets to wire racks to cool. Allow to cool thoroughly before frosting.
4. Whisk butter, confectioners' sugar, and 1 tsp. vanilla in a small bowl until no lumps remain. Whisk in milk, 1 tbsp. per batch, until mixture achieves desired spreading consistency. Whisk in food coloring to have desired color. Frost cooled cookies. Place cookies on waxed paper to set.

Nutrition Information

Calories: 133 calories; Total Carbohydrate: 20.6g Cholesterol: 11 mg Total Fat: 5.2g Proteinr: 1.3g Sodium: 82 mg

PUMPKIN COOKIE CUPS

Serving: 32 - **Prep:** 30m - **Ready in:** 1h40m

INGREDIENTS

- 2 cups all-purpose flour
- 1 1/2 tsps. baking powder
- 1/2 tsp. salt
- 1/4 tsp.ground nutmeg (optional)
- 1/2 cup unsalted butter, softened
- 1 cup white sugar
- 1 egg
- 2 tbsps. milk
- 1 (3 oz.) package cream cheese, softened

- 1 cup confectioners' sugar, divided
- 1/3 cup pumpkin puree
- 2 3/4 cups confectioners' sugar
- 1 1/2 tsps.ground cinnamon
- 1/4 tsp.ground nutmeg
- 1/4 tsp.groundginger
- 1 pinchground cloves

DIRECTION

1. Heat oven to 200°C (400°F) beforehand.greasing 32 miniature muffin cups.
2. In a bowl, sift a quarter tsp. of nutmeg, salt, baking powder, and flour. Using an electric mixer to cream sugar with unsalted butter in the second large mixing bowl till workable and smooth; beating in milk and egg. Setting the mixer to low speed and beating in flour mixturegradually, beat just till the dough comes together.
3. Pinching off dough by tbsp., rolling into a ball; in the prepared mini muffin cups, place balls.
4. In the preheated oven, allow to bake for 8-10 minutes till edges begin to turngolden brown. Removing from oven; allow to rest for a minute. Pressing a small depression into the top of each cookie with the back of a rounded tsp. measure. Before removing to finish cooling down on a rack, allow cookies to cool in pan for 5 minutes. It willgive the cookies a little twist when you lift them out.
5. In a bowl, using an electric mixer for beating a cup of confectioners' sugar with cream cheese till smooth. Beating in pumpkin puree slowly till mixed thoroughly. Beating in 2 and 3/4 cups of the remaining confectioners' sugar, a little at a time. Stirring in a pinch of cloves, a quarter tsp. ofginger, a quarter tsp. of nutmeg, and cinnamon. In every cookie cup, piping or spooning the pumpkin mixture.

Nutrition Information
Calories: 149 calories; Total Carbohydrate: 27.4g Cholesterol: 16 mg Total Fat: 4.1g Proteinr: 1.3g Sodium: 77 mg

DROP SUGAR COOKIES II

Serving: 236 - **Prep:** 15m - **Ready in:** 1h

INGREDIENTS

- 2 cups butter, softened
- 2 1/2 cups shortening
- 12 cups white sugar

- 18 eggs
- 2 tbsps. vanilla extract
- 24 cups all-purpose flour
- 2 tbsps. baking soda
- 2 tbsps. salt
- 4 1/2 cups sour milk

DIRECTION

1. Turn on the oven to 350°F (175°C) to preheat. Use parchment paper to line baking sheets. Beat together white sugar, shortening and butter in a large bowl until smooth. Whip in a few eggs at a time, and mix in the vanilla. Mix together salt, baking soda and flour; mix the sour cream and the dry mixture alternating into the creamed mixture. Scoop out cookies with a 1/4 cup measure or a size 16 cookie scoop onto the prepped cookie sheets. Arrange them at least 3 inches apart from each other. Put a couple into the oven to test how much they spread, and see it they have to be patted before baking.

2. Put into the prepped oven to bake until the bottoms start to turngolden for 10 to 12 minutes. Allow to cool on baking sheets.

Nutrition Information

Calories: 126 calories; Total Carbohydrate: 20.1g Cholesterol: 19 mg Total Fat: 4.3g Proteinr: 2g Sodium: 111 mg

EASYGRAHAM CRACKER COOKIES

Serving: 12 - **Prep:** 20m - **Ready in:** 30m

INGREDIENTS

- 1/2 cup white sugar
- 1/2 cup packed brown sugar
- 1/2 cup butter, softened
- 1 egg
- 1 1/2 cups all-purpose flour
- 1/2 tsp. baking soda
- 1/2 tsp. salt
- 1/2 cup chocolate chips, or to taste (optional)
- 4graham crackers, crushed

DIRECTION

1. Heat the oven to 190 ° C or 375 ° F.
2. In a big bowl, whip egg, butter, brown sugar and white sugar. Mix baking soda, salt and flour to mixture of sugar just to mix the batter; fold chocolate chips in. Form dough to an-inch balls.
3. Place thegraham cracker crumbs in a sealable bag. Put every dough ball in bag, 1 by 1, and shake to coat fully ingraham cracker crumbs. Place the coated balls of dough onto baking sheet.
4. Bake in prepped oven for 10 minutes till cookies edges turn pale brown and show 'cracks' in the center.

Nutrition Information

Calories: 241 calories; Total Carbohydrate: 35.5g Cholesterol: 36 mg Total Fat: 10.6g Proteinr: 2.7g Sodium: 227 mg

EASY SUGAR COOKIES

Serving: 48 - **Prep:** 15m - **Ready in:** 25m

INGREDIENTS

- 2 3/4 cups all-purpose flour
- 1 tsp. baking soda
- 1/2 tsp. baking powder
- 1 cup butter, softened
- 1 1/2 cups white sugar
- 1 egg
- 1 tsp. vanilla extract

DIRECTION

1. Set an oven to 190°C (375°F) and start preheating. Stir baking powder, baking soda, and flour in a small bowl. Then put aside.
2. Cream sugar and butter together in a large bowl until they become smooth. Whisk in vanilla and egg. Combine in the dry ingredientsgradually. Roll rounded teaspoonfuls of dough to form into balls, then transfer onto ungreased cookie sheets.
3. In the prepared oven, bake untilgolden, or for 8-10 minutes. Allow to stand on the cookie sheet for 2 minutes, then transfer onto wire racks to cool.

Nutrition Information

Calories: 86 calories; Total Carbohydrate: 11.7g Cholesterol: 14 mg Total Fat: 4g Proteinr: 0.9g Sodium: 60 mg

EGG YOLK PAINTED CHRISTMAS COOKIES

Serving: 24 - **Prep:** 10m - **Ready in:** 1h25m

INGREDIENTS

- 1/2 cup butter, softened
- 1/2 cup shortening
- 1 cup sifted confectioners' sugar
- 1 egg
- 1 tsp. vanilla extract
- 2 1/2 cups all-purpose flour
- 1 tsp. salt
- 1 egg yolk
- 1/4 tsp. water
- assorted colors of paste food coloring

DIRECTION

1. Cream shortening and margarine or butter; slowly put in the sugar, whipping till fluffy and light. Put in the vanilla and egg; whip thoroughly.
2. Mix salt and flour; mix into the creamed mixture. Split the dough in half; refrigerate with cover for not less than 1 hour.
3. Unroll a dough portion on a cookie sheet slightly dusted with flour into thickness of 1/8 inch. Use with assorted cutters to cut dough out; take the dough trimmings. Use small paintbrush and Egg Yolk Paint to paint various patterns over cookies. Bake about 9 to 10 minutes, at 190 ° C or 375 ° F. Transfer onto wire racks and let cool. Redo the process with the rest of the dough.
4. Prep Egg Yolk Paint: mix water and egg yolk; combine thoroughly. Distribute mixture to a few custard cups; color as wished using paste food coloring. Put on cover till set to use. Put several drops of water in case paint thickens, and stir thoroughly. Makes 1 1/2 tbsps..

Nutrition Information

Calories: 145 calories; Total Carbohydrate: 15.2g Cholesterol: 26 mg Total Fat: 8.6g Proteinr: 1.8g Sodium: 128 mg

GOLDEN HONEY SNAPS

Serving: 12 - **Prep:** 20m - **Ready in:** 30m

INGREDIENTS

- 1/2 cup butter, softened
- 1/4 cup honey
- 3 tbsps.golden syrup
- 1 tsp. baking soda
- 1 cup all-purpose flour
- 1/2 cup white sugar

DIRECTION

1. Set the oven at 350°F (175°C) and start preheating. Use parchment paper to line a baking sheet.
2. In a saucepan, mixgolden syrup, honey and butter together. Cook while stirring the mixture frequently over medium heat, till the ingredients are well-blended and the butter is melted. Mix in baking soda; take away from the heat.
3. In a mixing bowl, measure sugar and flour; stir to blend. Transfer the butter mixture into the bowl with the flour; combine till blended evenly. Shape the dough into 1 in. balls; arrange on the prepared baking sheet.
4. Bake for 10-12 minutes in the preheated oven, or tillgolden brown. Allow to cool for a few minutes on the baking sheet; then, take away and let cool completely on a wire rack.

Nutrition Information

Calories: 174 calories; Total Carbohydrate: 25.9g Cholesterol: 20 mg Total Fat: 7.8g Proteinr: 1.2g Sodium: 163 mg

GOOD-AS-GRANDMA'S SUGAR COOKIES

Serving: 36

INGREDIENTS

- 1 cup butter, softened
- 1 cup white sugar
- 1 egg
- 3 tsps. milk
- 1 tsp. vanilla extract
- 3 cups all-purpose flour
- 1 1/2 tsps. baking powder
- 1/2 tsp. salt

DIRECTION

1. Turn on the oven to 400°F (205°C) to preheat. Use parchment paper to line baking sheets. Beat together sugar and butter until fluffy and light. Whip in vanilla, milk and egg. Sift together the salt, baking powder and flour. Combine butter mixture and flour mixture until mixed. On the prepared baking sheets, drop dough by teaspoonfuls and put into the oven to bake until justgolden or for 5 to 8 minutes at 400°F (205°C).

Nutrition Information

Calories: 107 calories; Total Carbohydrate: 13.6g Cholesterol: 19 mg Total Fat: 5.4g Proteinr: 1.3g Sodium: 91 mg

GRAM OPAL'S SUGAR COOKIES

Serving: 24 - **Prep:** 15m - **Ready in:** 20m

INGREDIENTS

- 2 1/3 cups all-purpose flour
- 1 tsp. baking soda
- 1/8 tsp. salt
- 1 cup butter
- 1 cup white sugar
- 1 egg
- 1 tsp. vanilla extract
- 1/2 tsp. lemon extract

Icing:

- 2 cups confectioners' sugar

- 1/4 cup butter, melted
- 1 tbsp. hot water, or as needed
- 1/2 tsp. vanilla extract
- 24 whole pecans

DIRECTION

1. Preheat an oven to 175°C/350°F thengrease 2 baking sheets.
2. Sift 1/8 tsp. salt, baking soda and flour in bowl.
3. Use electric mixer to beat egg, white sugar and 1 cup butter for 2-3 minutes till creamy. Add lemon extract, vanilla extract and flour mixture to butter mixture; mix till dough is blended well. Roll cookie dough to walnut-sized balls; put on prepped cookie sheets, 2-in. apart. Use bottom ofglass to press each ball down to slightly flatten.
4. In preheated oven, bake for 6-7 minutes till baked through; cool.
5. Mix vanilla, hot water, 1/4 cup melted butter and confectioners' sugar till icing is smooth and sugar fully dissolves in a bowl; spread icing over cooled cookies. Put pecan on each cookie.

Nutrition Information

Calories: 216 calories; Total Carbohydrate: 28.3g Cholesterol: 33 mg Total Fat: 11g Proteinr: 1.8g Sodium: 136 mg

GRANDMA MINNIE'S OLD FASHIONED SUGAR COOKIE S

Serving: 78 - **Prep:** 20m - **Ready in:** 28m

INGREDIENTS

- 3 cups sifted all-purpose flour
- 1 1/2 tsps. baking powder
- 1/2 tsp. salt
- 1 cup white sugar
- 1 cup butter
- 1 egg, lightly beaten
- 3 tbsps. cream
- 1 tsp. vanilla extract

DIRECTION

1. Start preheating the oven to 400°F (200°C).
2. Sift sugar, salt, baking powder, all-purpose flour together over a large bowl. Cut in the butter then using a pastry blender, blend until the mixture resembles cornmeal. Mix in the vanilla, cream and lightly beaten egg. Blend well. If desired, chill the dough.
3. Roll out the dough to 1/8-in. thickness on floured surface. Drizzle over with sugar. Slice into the preferred shapes. Place into unoiled baking sheets.
4. Bake until delicately brown, or about 6-8 mins.

Nutrition Information

Calories: 51 calories; Total Carbohydrate: 6.3g Cholesterol: 9 mg Total Fat: 2.7g Proteinr: 0.6g Sodium: 40 mg

GRANDMA SHEETS' SUGAR COOKIES

Serving: 48

INGREDIENTS

*   2 cups white sugar
*   1 cup shortening
*   2 tsps. baking powder
*   1 tsp.ground nutmeg
*   3 eggs
*   1 cup milk
*   1 tsp. baking soda
*   5 cups all-purpose flour

DIRECTION

1. Combine together theground nutmeg, sugar, baking powder, and shortening. Beat eggs and then add to the mixture. Mix baking soda and milk and add to the mixture. Pour in flour. In the beginning, start out with agood mixer but switch to hand-mixing once the dough becomes too thick as you add enough flour to prevent the dough from becoming too sticky. Roll out the dough to about 1/4 inch or so.
2. Pour flour onto the dough, counter and rolling pin. You can chill the dough for about 15 minutes in case you live in a very humid place. You can chill the portion of dough not using any time soon. Roll the dough out to 1/4 inch. Chop out using any cookie cutter and then transfer to cookie sheet.

3. Bake for about 8 minutes in a preheated oven 175 degrees C (350 degrees F) or until browned lightly around edges or at the bottom. Remove from the sheets and then transfer to cool on wire racks or flattened grocery bags .

Nutrition Information

Calories: 125 calories; Total Carbohydrate: 18.6g Cholesterol: 12 mg Total Fat: 4.8g Proteinr: 1.9g Sodium: 53 mg

GRANDMA TIBBITTS SUGAR COOKIES

Serving: 24 - **Prep:** 20m - **Ready in:** 30m

INGREDIENTS

- 1 cup lard
- 2 cups white sugar
- 2 eggs
- 1 cup buttermilk
- 4 cups all-purpose flour
- 1 tsp. baking soda
- 1 tsp.ground nutmeg
- 1 tsp. salt

DIRECTION

1. Set oven to 400°F (200°C) to preheat. Lightly butter cookie sheets.
2. Beat sugar and lard together in a large mixing bowl. Beat in eggs, one by one; whisk in buttermilk until mixture looks very runny. Mix salt, nutmeg, baking soda, and flour together; mix into buttermilk mixture using a wooden spoon by your hand. Do not overwork the dough as it will make cookies become dense. Drop cookie dough onto thegreased cookie sheets by spoonfuls. For cut out cookies, chill dough in the fridge for a few hours. Flatten dough to 1/2-inch thick and cut dough and coat your cookie cutter with flour after each cut.
3. Bake cookies in the preheated oven for 8 to 10 minutes. Let cool for 5 minutes on the baking sheet before transferring to a wire rack to cool entirely.

Nutrition Information

Calories: 228 calories; Total Carbohydrate: 33.1g Cholesterol: 24 mg Total Fat: 9.3g Proteinr: 3g Sodium: 166 mg

GRANDMA'S CUTOUT SUGAR COOKIES

Serving: 72 - **Prep:** 10m - **Ready in:** 3h16m

INGREDIENTS

- 2 cups butter
- 1 1/2 cups white sugar
- 3 eggs
- 1 tsp. vanilla extract
- 1 tsp. almond extract (optional)
- 3 1/2 cups all-purpose flour
- 2 tsps. cream of tartar
- 1 tsp. baking soda
- 1/2 tsp. salt

DIRECTION

1. Use an electric mixer to whip sugar and butter in a big bowl till smooth. Put in the initial egg while whipping continuously, completely blending the egg prior to putting another one and completely whipping to the mixture. Whip almond extract and vanilla extract into mixture including the third egg.
2. In another bowl, stir together the salt, baking soda, cream of tartar and flour; put into wet mixture and whip to just combine wet and dry and form into a cookie dough. Collect dough to a ball, encase with plastic wrap, and chill till cold, for not less than 3 hours.
3. Heat the oven to 175 ° C or 350 ° F.
4. Unroll dough on a floured counter and use cookie cutters to cut dough. Place the cut cookies on baking sheets.
5. Let cookies bake for 6 to 8 minutes in prepped oven till starting to brown on edges' surrounding.

Nutrition Information

Calories: 87 calories; Total Carbohydrate: 8.9g Cholesterol: 21 mg Total Fat: 5.4g Proteinr: 0.9g Sodium: 73 mg

GRANDMA'S OLD FASHIONED TEA CAKES

Serving: 24 - **Prep:** 45m - **Ready in:** 53m

INGREDIENTS

- 1 cup butter
- 1 3/4 cups white sugar
- 2 eggs
- 3 cups all-purpose flour
- 1/2 tsp. baking soda
- 1/2 tsp. salt
- 1/4 tsp.ground nutmeg
- 1 tsp. vanilla extract

DIRECTION

1. Cream sugar and butter in one medium-sized bowl, till smooth. Whip in eggs, one by one, then mix in vanilla. Mix nutmeg, salt, baking soda and flour; put into creamed mixture, stir. Work the dough on a board dusted with flour, a couple of turns till smooth. Chill with cover till set.
2. Heat an oven to 165 °C or 325 °F. Unroll dough on a slightly floured counter into thickness of 1/4 inch. Use preferred cookie cutters shapes to cut the dough. Arrange the cookies on cookie sheets 1 1/2-inch away.
3. Bake in prepped oven, about 8 to 10 minutes. Cool cookies for 5 minutes on baking sheet then remove onto wire rack and fully cool.

Nutrition Information

Calories: 188 calories; Total Carbohydrate: 26.6g Cholesterol: 36 mg Total Fat: 8.3g Proteinr: 2.2g Sodium: 135 mg

GRANDMOTHER'S BROWN SUGAR COOKIES

Serving: 24

INGREDIENTS

- 3 cups packed brown sugar
- 3/4 cup shortening
- 3/4 tsp. cream of tartar
- 4 eggs
- 1 tsp. vanilla extract

- 5 cups all-purpose flour
- 3/4 tsp. baking soda

DIRECTION

1. Turn oven to 400°F (200°C) to preheat.
2. Beat eggs, shortening, and sugar together. Mix in vanilla until combined.
3. Mix cream of tartar, baking soda, and flour together in another mixing bowl; mix into brown sugar mixture until a soft dough forms.
4. Roll dough out, cut with cookie cutters and bake in the preheated oven for 8 to 10 minutes .

Nutrition Information

Calories: 269 calories; Total Carbohydrate: 47g Cholesterol: 31 mg Total Fat: 7.5g Proteinr: 3.8g Sodium: 59 mg

GREATGRANDAD'S SUGAR COOKIES

Serving: 30 - **Prep:** 30m - **Ready in:** 1h10m

INGREDIENTS

- 6 cups all-purpose flour
- 1 tbsp. baking powder
- 1 tsp.ground nutmeg
- 1 pinch salt
- 2 1/2 cups white sugar
- 1 1/2 cups shortening
- 1 tsp. baking soda
- 1 cup sour milk
- 3 eggs, beaten
- 1 tsp. vanilla extract

DIRECTION

1. Preheat the oven to 350°F (175°C). Use a parchment paper to line cookie sheets.
2. Mix the nutmeg, 4 cups of flour, sugar, baking powder and salt together in a medium-sized bowl. Mash the shortening into the mixture until the texture is like that of coarse crumbs. Add in the beaten eggs, baking soda, vanilla and sour milk and mix everything together. Mix the mixture as little as you can, and put in the remaining flour if need be to turn the dough thick enough to unroll.

3. Roll dough out onto a surface that is slightly covered with flour until it is 1/4 inch in thickness. Use cookie cutters to cut the flattened dough into whatever shape you like. On the prepared cookie sheets, put in the cut-out cookies 1 inch away from each other.

4. Put it in the preheated oven and let it bake for 8-10 minutes. Allow the baked cookies to cool down on the cookie sheets.

Nutrition Information

Calories: 258 calories; Total Carbohydrate: 36.4g Cholesterol: 19 mg Total Fat: 11.1g Proteinr: 3.5g Sodium: 107 mg

HEALTHIER (BUT STILL) THE BEST ROLLED SUGAR COOKIES

Serving: 60 - **Prep:** 20m - **Ready in:** 1h28m

INGREDIENTS

- 1 1/2 cups butter, softened
- 1 cupgranular sucralose sweetener (such as Splenda)
- 1/3 cup white sugar
- 4 eggs
- 1 tsp. vanilla extract
- 5 cups all-purpose flour
- 2 tsps. baking powder

DIRECTION

1. In a big bowl, cream together the sugar, sweetener and butter until smooth. Beat in vanilla extract and eggs, then stir in baking powder and flour. Put cover on and chill the dough for a minimum of 1 hour or overnight.

2. Set an oven to preheat to 200°C (400°F).

3. On a floured surface, roll out the dough to 1/4- to 1/2-inch thick. Use any cookie cutter to cut it into shapes. On ungreased baking trays, put the cookies 1 inch apart .

4. Bake for about 6-8 minutes in the preheated oven until they turngolden. Allow to completely cool.

Nutrition Information

Calories: 88 calories; Total Carbohydrate: 9.3g Cholesterol: 25 mg Total Fat: 5g Proteinr: 1.5g Sodium: 54 mg

HOLIDAY COOKIE CUTOUTS

Serving: 32 - **Ready in:** 3h

INGREDIENTS

- 1⅔ cups all-purpose flour
- ¾ cup whole-wheat flour
- 1 tsp. baking powder
- ¼ tsp. salt
- ⅓ cup low-fat firm silken tofu, (see Ingredient note)
- 1 large egg
- 1 cup sugar
- ¼ cup canola oil
- 1 tbsp. butter, softened
- 2 tsps. vanilla extract
- Cinnamon-Sugar Topping, or Decorator Icing (recipes follow)

DIRECTION

1. In a medium bowl, combine salt, baking powder, whole-wheat flour, and all-purpose flour.
2. Blend tofu into puree in a food processor. Put in vanilla, butter, oil, sugar, and egg; pulse until no lumps remain, stopping and scraping down the sides of the work bowl once or twice. Put in dry ingredients; process until incorporated.
3. Turn dough onto a work surface lightly coated with flour; knead dough several times. Cut dough into 2 portions; flatten each piece of dough into a disk. Sprinkle flour over the disks; wrap the disks in plastic wrap. Chill dough in the fridge for a minimum of 2 hours or overnight.
4. Set oven to 350°F to preheat.grease several baking sheets with cooking spray or line them with parchment paper.
5. Roll dough slightly less than 1/4-inch thick on a work surface lightly coated with flour, working with 1 portion at a time. Use a cookie cutter to cut out shapes. Accumulate scraps and re-roll. Arrange cookies approximately 1/2 inch apart on the prepared baking sheets. Sprinkle top with cinnamon-sugar topping (if using).
6. Bake cookies for 12 to 16 minutes in the preheated oven, one sheet at a time, until edges turn lightgolden. Remove cookies to a wire rack and allow to cool thoroughly.
7. Garnish cookies as desired in case you use Decorator Icing. Allow to sit for about 30 to 45 minutes or until frosting is hardened.

Calories: 85 calories; Total Carbohydrate: 14g Cholesterol: 7 mg Total Fat: 2g Fiber: 1g Proteinr: 2g Sodium: 36 mg Sugar: 7g Saturated Fat: 0g

ICED SUGAR CUT-OUT COOKIES

Serving: 36 - **Ready in:** 2h45m

INGREDIENTS

- Cookie Dough
- 2 cups all-purpose flour, plus more if needed
- ⅔ cup white whole-wheat flour (see Tips)
- 1½ tsps. baking powder
- ¼ tsp. salt
- ⅓ cup canola oil or corn oil
- 4 tbsps. unsalted butter, slightly softened
- ½ cup plus 1 tbsp.granulated sugar
- 1 large egg
- Finelygrated zest of 1 medium lemon
- ¼ cup plus 1 tbsp. honey
- 2½ tsps. vanilla extract
- ½ tsp. almond extract or lemon extract
- Cookie Icing
- 2 cups confectioners' sugar, plus more as needed
- 2 tbsps. dried egg whites (see Tips)
- 4 tbsps. water
- 1 tsp. light corn syrup
- ½ tsp. vanilla or almond extract
- "Holiday" red natural liquid dye (see Tips)
- Green natural liquid dye (see Tips)

DIRECTION

1. Prep cookie dough: in one medium bowl, mix salt, baking powder, whole-wheat flour and all-purpose flour. Whip lemon zest, egg,granulated sugar, butter and oil at low speed of an electric mixer in a mixing bowl to blend thoroughly. Whip in vanilla, almond (or lemon) extract and honey, to incorporate evenly.

2. Whip approximately 1/2 of flour mixture into wet ingredients on low speed of mixer, then moderate speed, to incorporate. Whip in the rest of the flour mixture barely to incorporate.

3. Split dough into 3 portions. Put a portion on a parchment paper sheet with length of 12-inch and form into disk. Put another parchment sheet on top. Unroll dough between parchments into circle of 8-inches with quarter-inch thickness. Put dough in paper onto baking sheet. Redo with the rest of dough. Place into freezer on baking sheet for not less than half an hour to a day till firm and cold. Put one more baking sheet in freezer to also chill, you will use this beneath dough as cookies are cut out.

4. To form and bake the cookies: place one rack in center of oven; heat the oven to 350°F. Line parchment paper on a big baking sheet(s).

5. Take out of freezer and put on cold baking sheet a dough portion at a time. Peel off top parchment sheet and use 2 1/2- to 3-inches cookie cutters to cut out cookies. Remove to a prepped baking sheet using a thin, wide spatula, with approximately 1 1/2-inch spaces. Redo with the rest of the dough. Freeze dough if itgets very soft till firm once more. Put the trimmings aside as you cut out the cookies. Form all the trimming back into a flat round and roll once more between sheets of parchment. Freeze for not less than half an hour then cut it out.

6. Let cookies bake for 6 to 12 minutes on the middle rack, a pan at each time, to brown the underside. Rest for five minutes, then remove onto the wire racks and let cool.

7. To prep frosting and jazz the cookies up: in one small bowl, mix dried egg whites and confectioners' sugar. Mix in corn syrup, vanilla (or almond) extract and water till smooth. Distribute the frosting between three small bowls. Put a couple drops ofgreen dye to one and red dye to the other, having white, red andgreen frosting.

8. Pipe the frosting: put a bit more confectioners' sugar as necessary to stiffen frosting for piping. Scoop every frosting in small plastic bag with a small tip of a corner cut off or to a pastry bag fitted with writing tip. Pipe vibrant designs on cooled cookies.

9. For "wet on wet" frosting: if need be, add a bit more water to thingreen frosting to have a spreadable consistency. Smeargreen icing on cooled cookies using a butter knife or small paintbrush. Pipe red or white design on top ofgreen frosting while frosting is still wet. Run a toothpick through frosting to mix the colors.

Nutrition Information

Calories: 115 calories; Total Carbohydrate: 19 g Cholesterol: 9 mg Total Fat: 4g Fiber: 0g Proteinr: 2g Sodium: 44 mg Sugar: 12g Saturated Fat: 1g

IRISH CREAM SUGAR COOKIES

Serving: 48 - **Prep:** 30m - **Ready in:** 2h36m

INGREDIENTS

- 1 cup butter, softened
- 1 1/2 cups white sugar
- 1 tsp. vanilla extract
- 1 egg yolk
- 1 egg
- 1/2 cup Irish cream liqueur
- 4 cups all-purpose flour
- 1/2 tsp. salt
- 1 tbsp. baking powder

DIRECTION

1. Beat sugar and butter until fluffy. Whip in egg yolk and vanilla until blended; whip in egg and blend until the mixture is smooth. Put in Irish cream; beat until blended.
2. Sift baking powder, salt and flour. Mix into butter mixture until well combined. Shape into a flat ball; use plastic wrap to thoroughly wrap and chill for two hours or overnight.
3. Set oven to 175°C (350°F) and start preheating. Use parchment paper to line 2 baking sheets.
4. On a work surface dusted with flour, roll out dough until 1/4-inch thick. Use cookie cutters to cut out shapes; arrange onto the baking sheets.
5. Bake for 6-8 minutes at 175°C (350°F) until around edges turngolden brown. Place on a wire rack to cool to room temperature.

Nutrition Information

Calories: 108 calories; Total Carbohydrate: 15.5g Cholesterol: 18 mg Total Fat: 4.1g Proteinr: 1.3g Sodium: 84 mg

ROLLED SUGAR COOKIES

Serving: 36

INGREDIENTS

- Reynolds Parchment Paper
- 2 1/2 cups all-purpose flour
- 1 1/2 tsps. baking powder
- 1/4 tsp. salt
- 1 cup unsalted butter, softened
- 3/4 cup sugar
- 2 large egg yolks
- 1 tsp. vanilla extract

DIRECTION

1. In a large mixing bowl, mix salt, baking powder, and flour together; put to one side.
2. Beat sugar and butter with an electric mixer for about 3 minutes or until fluffy. Beat in vanilla and egg yolks. Slowly beat in flour mixture until incorporated.
3. Use parchment paper to wrap dough; place wrapped dough in Hefty slider bag; chill for about 1 hour or until deep cold.
4. Set oven to 350°F to preheat. Place Reynold parchment paper on cookie sheets; put to one side.
5. Roll dough out to a thickness of 1/8 inch between 2 sheets of parchment paper lightly dusted with flour; use 2-inch cookie cutters to cut dough. Arrange dough on cookie sheets lined with parchment papers .
6. Bake cookies in the preheated oven until edges turn brown lightly, for 6 to 8 minutes. Remove parchment paper with cookies to cooling rack to cool.
7. Garnish cookies if desired. Keep cookies in an airtight container for a maximum of 5 days.

Nutrition Information

Calories: 96 calories; Total Carbohydrate: 10.9g Cholesterol: 25 mg Total Fat: 5.4g Proteinr: 1.1g Sodium: 38 mg

LEMON-BLUEBERRY CHEESECAKE COOKIES

Serving: 18 - **Prep:** 15m - **Ready in:** 25m

INGREDIENTS

- 1 (8 oz.) package cream cheese, softened
- 1 egg
- 1 (17.5 oz.) pouch sugar cookie mix (such as Betty Crocker)

- 4 tsps. lemon extract
- 2/3 cup blueberry baking chips (such as The Prepared Pantry)

DIRECTION

1. Turn on the oven to 350°F (175°C) to preheat. Use parchment paper to line 2 baking pans.
2. In a bowl, thoroughly beat cream cheese until it is smooth. Stir in egg to well-combined. Stir in lemon extract and sugar cookie mix until the dough blends well. Add blueberry chips and foldgently.
3. Arrange tablespoonfusl of dough on baking sheets, each 2 inches away from another. Pat each cookie dollop down lightly.
4. Put into the oven to bake for 9-12 minutes for the edges to turn lightgolden. Cool to serve.

Nutrition Information

Calories: 220 calories; Total Carbohydrate: 27.4g Cholesterol: 24 mg Total Fat: 11.1g Proteinr: 2.3g Sodium: 107 mg

LIPARDO'S PUTO SECO

Serving: 12 - **Prep:** 10m - **Ready in:** 50m

INGREDIENTS

- 1 egg
- 1/3 cup white sugar
- 1/4 cup butter, softened
- 1 cup all-purpose flour
- 1 cup cornstarch
- 1/2 cup powdered milk
- 1/2 tsp. baking powder
- 1 dash salt

DIRECTION

1. Prepare the oven by preheating to 375°F (190°C). Prepare a baking sheet that isgreased. In a bowl, mix salt, baking powder, powdered milk, cornstarch, flour, butter, white sugar, and egg. Massage for several few minutes to form a soft dough. Split the dough in 12 pieces. Then turn each piece in a ball and slightly flatten. Set 1 inch apart on prepared baking sheet.
2. Place in preheated oven and bake for approximately 10 minutes until light brown. Let it fully cool and keep in an airtight container.

Nutrition Information

Calories: 166 calories ; Total Carbohydrate: 25.4g Cholesterol: 31 mg Total Fat: 5.8g Proteinr: 3.1g

Sodium: 101 mg

LOFTHOUSE SUGAR COOKIE RIP-OFF

Serving: 36 - **Prep:** 15m - **Ready in:** 8h33m

INGREDIENTS

- 2 cups white sugar
- 1 cup butter, softened
- 3 eggs
- 1 1/2 cups sour cream
- 1 1/2 tsps. vanilla extract
- 5 cups all-purpose flour, or more as needed
- 1 tsp. baking powder
- 1 tsp. baking soda

DIRECTION

1. Use an electric mixer to whip butter and sugar till smooth in a big bowl. Put in the eggs one by one, blending every egg into butter mixture prior to putting the next. Whip vanilla extract and sour cream along with the final egg.
2. In another bowl, combine baking soda, baking powder and 5 cups flour; whip along with creamy mixture barely to incorporate into dough. Use plastic wrap to cover the bowl and chill for 8 hours up to overnight.
3. Heat the oven to 220 ° C or 425 ° F. Line parchment paper on baking sheets.
4. Transfer dough out to a waxed paper sheet dusted with flour on an even work counter. Dust top of dough with flour and place one more waxed paper sheet over dough. Unroll dough into thickness of 1/4- to 3/8-inch, prevent dough from adhering and to reach the best rolling consistency with more flour. Use preferred cookie cutters shapes to cut the rolled dough and place on prepped baking sheets.
5. Bake for 8 minutes in prepped oven till firm on the edges. Let cookies cool for 10 minutes on baking sheet then remove onto wire rack and fully cool.

Nutrition Information

Calories: 178 calories; Total Carbohydrate: 24.9g Cholesterol: 33 mg Total Fat: 7.7g Proteinr: 2.7g

Sodium: 96 mg

LOLLIPOP SUGAR COOKIES

Serving: 24 - **Prep:** 20m - **Ready in:** 30m

INGREDIENTS

- 1 cup shortening
- 1/2 cup white sugar
- 1/2 cup brown sugar
- 1/2 tsp. vanilla
- 1 egg
- 2 cups all-purpose flour
- 1/2 tsp. baking soda
- 1/2 tsp. salt

DIRECTION

1. Set oven to preheat at 350°F (175°C).
2. Cream brown sugar, white sugar and shortening in a medium bowl. Whisk in vanilla and egg. Mix flour, salt and baking soda; add it into the cream mixture and mix. Mold dough into balls the size of walnuts. Insert craft sticks into the middle of each ball. Arrange the balls 3 inches apart on an ungreased cookie sheet, making sure the sticks are parallel to the cookie sheet. Using a glass dipped it sugar, flatten the balls lightly. You can now garnish with colored sugar or sprinkles, as you wish.
3. Bake in the oven for 8-10 minutes. Let them cool for 5 minutes on the baking sheet. Transfer to a wire rack to cool fully. Once cool, wrap with plastic wrap and tie with a ribbon.

Nutrition Information

Calories: 146 calories; Total Carbohydrate: 15.1g Cholesterol: 14 mg Total Fat: 8.9g Proteinr: 1.3g Sodium: 78 mg

MA MA'S SUGAR COOKIES

Serving: 12 - **Prep:** 5m - **Ready in:** 15m

INGREDIENTS

- 1/2 cup butter flavored shortening
- 1 cup white sugar

- 2 eggs
- 1 tsp. vanilla extract
- 2 cups self-rising flour

DIRECTION

1. Turn on the oven to 350°F (175°C) to preheat.
2. Beat together sugar and shortening in a medium bowl. Beat in vanilla and eggs. Mix in self-rising flour to make a dough. Roll out the dough on a lightly floured surface so that it is 1/4-inch thick. Use cookie cutters to cut into desired shapes. On cookie sheets, arrange cookies 1 1/2 inches apart.
3. Put into the prepped oven to bake for 8-10 minutes. Let the cookies cool for 5 minutes on baking sheet; then let them cool completely on wire racks.

Nutrition Information

Calories: 230 calories; Total Carbohydrate: 32.2g Cholesterol: 31 mg Total Fat: 10g Proteinr: 3.1g Sodium: 276 mg

MAILAENDERLI

Serving: 50 - **Prep:** 50m - **Ready in:** 2h10m

INGREDIENTS

- 4 eggs
- 1 1/4 cups white sugar
- 1 1/8 cups butter, melted and cooled to lukewarm
- 1 pinch salt
- 4 cups all purpose flour
- 1 1/2 tsps.grated lemon zest
- 2 egg yolks, beaten
- seasonal colored sprinkles

DIRECTION

1. Whip eggs in one big bowl. Mix sugar in and whip for 10 minutes till mixture is pale and thick. Stir in the salt and melted butter. Slowly fold in lemon zest and flour. Chill with cover for not less than one hour or overnight preferably.
2. Heat the oven to 165 ° C or 325 ° F. Oil cookie sheet lightly.
3. Unroll dough on a floured counter to thickness of 1/4 inch. Cut to preferred forms with cookie cutters.

Arrange cookies on prepped cookie sheet. Brush with beaten egg yolks and jazz up using sprinkles.

4. Bake for about 15 to 20 minutes in prepped oven till edges turngolden. Let cookies cool onto racks .

Nutrition Information

Calories: 105 calories; Total Carbohydrate: 13.4g Cholesterol: 34 mg Total Fat: 5g Proteinr: 1.7g Sodium: 36 mg

MARY'S SUGAR COOKIES

Serving: 30 **- Prep:** 15m **- Ready in:** 2h25m

INGREDIENTS

- 1 cup butter, softened
- 1 1/2 cups sifted confectioners' sugar
- 1 egg
- 1 tsp. vanilla extract
- 1/2 tsp. almond extract
- 2 1/2 cups all-purpose flour
- 1 tsp. baking soda
- 1 tsp. cream of tartar
- 1/4 cupgranulated sugar for decoration

DIRECTION

1. Cream confectioners' sugar and butter together in a large bowl until smooth. Beat in egg and stir in almond extract and vanilla. Mix together cream of tartar, baking soda and flour; mix into the creamed mixture. Cover up and allow to chill for at least 2 hours.
2. Preheat the oven to 375°F (190°C). Separate the dough in two. On a lightly floured surface, roll each half out to the thickness of 3/16 inch. Use cookie cutter to cut into desired shapes. Ongreased cookie sheets, place the cookies 1 1/2 inches apart. Sprinkle plain or coloredgranulated sugar over the cookies.
3. Bake in the preheated oven for 8 minutes, until browned lightly. Cool on baking sheet for 5 minutes, then transfer to a wire rack for cooling completely.

Nutrition Information

Calories: 126 calories; Total Carbohydrate: 16g Cholesterol: 22 mg Total Fat: 6.4g Proteinr: 1.4g Sodium: 88 mg

MELT IN YOUR MOUTH COOKIES

Serving: 18 - **Prep:** 15m - **Ready in:** 1h25m

INGREDIENTS

- 1 cup butter
- 2 cups all-purpose flour
- 1 cup confectioners' sugar
- 1 pinch salt (optional)

DIRECTION

1. Mix together confectioners' sugar, flour and butter. It have the consistency of pie crust initially. Roll into one large log; use plastic wrap or wax paper to wrap. Let chill for one hour at least.
2. Turn on the oven to 350°F (175°C) to preheat.
3. Cut the cold log into slices of 1/4-inch thickness. On a baking sheet, arrange cookies. Put into the prepped oven to bake for 10 minutes until the edges barely start to turngolden. Keep an eye so they do not burn.

Nutrition Information

Calories: 167 calories; Total Carbohydrate: 17.2g Cholesterol: 27 mg Total Fat: 10.4g Proteinr: 1.5g Sodium: 82 mg

MELT-IN-YOUR-MOUTH SUGAR COOKIES

Serving: 48 - **Prep:** 35m - **Ready in:** 1h5m

INGREDIENTS

- ½ cup butter, softened
- ½ cup shortening
- 2 cups sugar
- 1 tsp. baking soda
- 1 tsp. cream of tartar
- ⅛ tsp. salt
- 3 egg yolks
- ½ tsp. vanilla

- 1¾ cups all-purpose flour

DIRECTION

1. Turn on the oven to 300 degrees F to preheat. Use an electric mixture to beat shortening and butter together in a large mixing bowl on medium to high speed for 30 seconds. Put in salt, cream of tartar, baking soda and sugar. Continue beating until mixed; scrape the sides of the bowl occasionally. Whip in vanilla and egg yolks. Use the mixer to beat in as much flour as you can. Add any remaining flour and stir.
2. Form balls of 1-inch with the dough. On ungreased parchment paper-lined cookie sheets, arrange balls 2 inches apart.
3. Put into the prepped oven to bake until the edges are set or for 12-14 minutes. Do not allow edges to brown. Let the cookies cool on cookie sheets for 2 minutes. Remove to wire racks to cool.

Nutrition Information

Calories: 88 calories; Total Carbohydrate: 12g Cholesterol: 18 mg Total Fat: 4g Fiber: 0g Proteinr: 1g Sodium: 47 mg Sugar: 8g Saturated Fat: 2g

MELTED SNOWMAN COOKIE

Serving: 12 - **Prep:** 1h - **Ready in:** 1h55m

INGREDIENTS

Sugar Cookie:
- 3/4 cup butter, softened
- 3/4 cup white sugar
- 1 tsp. baking powder
- 1/4 tsp. salt
- 1 egg
- 1 tbsp. milk
- 1 tsp. vanilla extract
- 2 cups all-purpose flour

Decorations:
- 12 large marshmallows
- 3 cups confectioners' sugar
- 1/4 cup water
- 1/2 cup chocolate chips

- 1 drop red food coloring, or as desired
- 1 drop yellow food coloring, or as desired

DIRECTION

1. Turn oven to 350°F (175°C) to preheat.
2. In a mixing bowl, beat butter for approximately 2 minutes with an electric mixer until fluffy. Whisk in salt, baking powder, and white sugar just until incorporated. Beat in vanilla extract, milk, and egg; mix in flour until just moistened. Chill the dough for approximately 10 minutes, covered with plastic wrap, until briefly chilled.
3. Spoon dough into balls slightly bigger thangolf balls; press into cookies. Place cookies on a baking sheet.
4. Bake cookies in the preheated oven until edges turngolden brown, for 10 to 20 minutes. Cool for 5 minutes on the baking sheet; transfer to a wire rack to cool entirely, for a minimum of half an hour .
5. Grease a microwaveable plate with butter. Arrange marshmallows on the buttered plate.
6. Microwave marshmallow for 10 to 15 seconds or until briefly puffed. Press marshmallow gently until bottoms ooze slightly.
7. In a mixing bowl, combine water and confectioners' sugar until icing is briefly thicker than drizzle-consistency. Stream icing over cookies and let it run down the edges, saving approximately 1 tbsp..
8. Melt chocolate chips for approximately half a minute in a ceramic or microwaveable glass bowl. Transfer melted chocolate to a plastic bag with a corner cut or a piping bag with a tiny tip.
9. Pat 1 marshmallow near an edge of each cookie to make the head of the snowman. Use melted chocolate to draw "stick arms" onto the icing.
10. Separate the reserved 1 tbsp. icing into 2 small mixing bowls. Color 1 bowl with orange food coloring and the other with red food coloring. garnish the snowmen with ties or scarves with yellow icing and red icing.

Nutrition Information

Calories: 412 calories; Total Carbohydrate: 70.1g Cholesterol: 46 mg Total Fat: 14.3g Proteinr: 3.3g Sodium: 185 mg

MELTING BISCUITS

Serving: 24

INGREDIENTS

- 1/2 cup butter, softened

- 3/8 cup white sugar
- 1 tsp. vanilla extract
- 1 egg yolk
- 1 cup self-rising flour
- 2 tbsps. cornstarch
- 1/4 tsp. salt
- 1/4 cup rolled oats

DIRECTION

1. Set oven to 375°F (190°C).grease cookie sheets.
2. Whip the butter with sugar until fluffy and light. Whip in the vanilla extract and egg yolk. Sift the salt, cornstarch, and flour together; mix into the butter mixture. Form dough into 20-24 small balls, about 1/2 inch in diameter. Roll each ball in the oats and put about 2-inch apart on cookie sheets.
3. Bake 15-20 minutes untilgolden brown. Cool on wire rack. Put in an airtight tin to store.

Nutrition Information

Calories: 73 calories; Total Carbohydrate: 8.2g Cholesterol: 19 mg Total Fat: 4.1g Proteinr: 0.8g Sodium: 118 mg

MEXICAN SUGAR COOKIES

Serving: 12

INGREDIENTS

- 2 1/2 cups shortening
- 1 cup white sugar
- 1 tsp. anise seed,ground
- 2 eggs
- 6 cups all-purpose flour
- 1 tbsp. baking powder
- 1/2 tbsp. cream of tartar
- 1/2 tsp. salt
- 1/4 cup orange juice
- 3 tbsps.ground cinnamon
- 1 cup white suga r

DIRECTION

1. Turn on the oven to 350°F (175°C) to preheat.
2. Beat shortening until fluffy and light. Put in anise seed and 1 cup of sugar. Stir well till creamy. Put in eggs; stir until well-mixed. Put in orange juice, salt, cream of tartar, baking powder and flour. Stir well.
3. Knead the dough until it is smoothened. Roll the dough to 1/2 inch thick on a lightly floured surface. Use cookie cutter to cut into different shapes. Put into the oven to bake for 5 to 8 minutes until they turn light brown in color. Roll cookies in the mixture of 3 tbsps. of cinnamon and 1 cup of sugar when they are still warm.

Nutrition Information

Calories: 755 calories; Total Carbohydrate: 83.6g Cholesterol: 31 mg Total Fat: 44.2g Proteinr: 7.6g Sodium: 232 mg

MINI CHIP SUGAR COOKIES

Serving: 18

INGREDIENTS

- 1/3 cup butter, softened
- 1/2 cup packed brown sugar
- 3/4 cup white sugar
- 1 egg
- 1 tsp. vanilla extract
- 2 cups all-purpose flour
- 1 tsp. baking soda
- 1/2 tsp. baking powder
- 1/2 tsp. salt
- 1/2 cup buttermilk
- 1 1/2 cups mini semi-sweet chocolate chips

DIRECTION

1. Set the oven to 350°F (175°C), and start preheating. Lightly coat a medium cookie sheet with oil.
2. In a large mixer bowl, cream sugar, brown sugar, margarine or butter until fluffy and light. Put in vanilla and egg; beat well. In another bowl, mix salt, baking powder, baking soda and flour; then put in alternately with buttermilk to make creamed mixture. Beat thoroughly. Mix in chips. Drop by rounded

tsps. onto the prepped cookie sheet.

3. Bake in the prepped oven until lightly browned, about 10-12 minutes. Take away from cookie sheet and allow to cool down.

Nutrition Information

Calories: 213 calories; Total Carbohydrate: 34.4g Cholesterol: 20 mg Total Fat: 8.2g Proteinr: 2.7g Sodium: 187 mg

MOLASSES SUGAR COOKIES I

Serving: 30

INGREDIENTS

- 3/4 cup butter flavored shortening
- 1 cup packed brown sugar
- 1 egg
- 1/4 cup molasses
- 2 cups all-purpose flour
- 1/4 tsp. salt
- 2 tsps. baking soda
- 1 tsp.ground cinnamon
- 1 tsp.ground cloves
- 1 tsp.groundginger

DIRECTION

1. Cream together the brown sugar and butter flavored shortening till fluffy and light. Put the molasses and egg and whisk thoroughly. Sift together theginger,ground cloves, cinnamon, baking soda, salt and flour. Put to the creamed mixture and combine thoroughly.
2. Refrigerate for a minimum of 1 hour or overnight.
3. Preheat an oven to 190°C or 375°F.
4. Roll into an-inch balls, roll in sugar. On ungreased cookie sheet, set the balls 2-inches away. Allow to bake for 10 minutes. Let slightly cool prior to taking off pan.

Nutrition Information

Calories: 116 calories; Total Carbohydrate: 15.8g Cholesterol: 6 mg Total Fat: 5.6g Proteinr: 1.1g Sodium: 109 mg

MOLASSES SUGAR COOKIES II

Serving: 36

INGREDIENTS

- 1 1/2 cups shortening
- 2 cups white sugar
- 1/2 cup molasses
- 2 eggs
- 4 cups all-purpose flour
- 4 tsps. baking soda
- 2 tsps.ground cinnamon
- 1 tsp. salt
- 1 tsp.ground cloves
- 1 tsp.groundginger

DIRECTION

1. Liquify the shortening and let cool. Put the molasses, eggs and sugar; beat thoroughly.
2. Sift theginger,ground cloves, salt, cinnamon, baking soda and flour. Put to molasses mixture and mix till well incorporated. Refrigerate the dough for a minimum of 3 hours or overnight.
3. Preheat an oven to 190°C or 375°F. Slightly oil a baking sheet.
4. Take dough off the refrigerator and shape into walnut-sized rounds. Roll rounds in white sugar. On the prepped baking sheet, put the rounds approximately 2 inches away.
5. Allow to bake in the preheated oven, for chewy cookies 8 to 10 minutes and for crisper cookies 10 to 12 minutes. Keep cookies in an airtight container.

Nutrition Information
Calories: 187 calories; Total Carbohydrate: 25.3g Cholesterol: 10 mg Total Fat: 9g Proteinr: 1.8g Sodium: 210 mg

MOM'S SUGAR COOKIES

Serving: 30

INGREDIENTS

- 1 cup butter
- 2 cups white sugar
- 3 eggs
- 4 1/2 cups sifted all-purpose flour
- 1 tsp. baking soda
- 1 tsp. cream of tartar
- 1/4 tsp. salt
- 1 tsp. vanilla extract

DIRECTION

1. Cream together sugar and butter; put in eggs. Run the dry ingredients 3 times through a sieve; mix together with the egg mixture thoroughly. Put in vanilla.
2. Roll in waxed paper to roll and put into the refrigerator to store and let it chill thoroughly.
3. Turn on the oven to 375°F (190°C) to preheat.
4. On well-floured board, roll out dough so that it is very thin. Use cookie cutter to cut. Put ongreased cookie sheets into the oven to bake for 6-10 minutes.

Nutrition Information

Calories: 182 calories; Total Carbohydrate: 27.8g Cholesterol: 35 mg Total Fat: 6.8g Proteinr: 2.6g Sodium: 112 mg

MORAVIAN SUGAR COOKIES

Serving: 30

INGREDIENTS

- 4 1/2 cups all-purpose flour
- 1/4 tsp. baking soda
- 1/4 tsp. salt
- 1 tsp.ground cinnamon
- 1/2 tsp.ground cloves
- 1/4 tsp.groundginger
- 1 cup packed brown sugar
- 1/2 cup butter
- 1/2 cup shortening

- 1 1/2 cups dark molasses
- 1/2 tsp. distilled white vinegar

DIRECTION

1. Combineginger, cloves, cinnamon, salt, baking soda and flour.
2. Beat shortening, butter and the brown sugar in another bowl. Put into the dry mixture and stir thoroughly. Put in vinegar and molasses. Stir thoroughly.
3. Refrigerate while covered overnight.
4. Roll out a little bit of dough to one-eighth (or less) inch thickness. Cut into shapes of your choice.
5. Bake in 180°C (350°F) oven until the cookies are lightly browned, about 10 minutes.

Nutrition Information

Calories: 201 calories; Total Carbohydrate: 33.9g Cholesterol: 8 mg Total Fat: 6.7g Proteinr: 2g Sodium: 60 mg

MRS. FIELDS SUGAR COOKIES

Serving: 18

INGREDIENTS

- 2 cups all-purpose flour
- 1/4 tsp. salt
- 3/4 cup white sugar
- 1 egg
- 1 tsp. vanilla extract
- 1/4 cup colored sugar for decoration
- 3/4 cup butter

DIRECTION

1. Preheat oven to 165°C or 325°F.
2. Use a wire whisk to combine salt and flour in a medium bowl. Use an electric mixer on medium speed to cream sugar and butter together in a large bowl. Beat in vanilla and egg until thoroughly blended. Scrape the sides of the bowl down, add flour mixture, and blend on low speed just until the mixture is combined. Be careful not to overmix.
3. Form the dough into a ball and flatten into a disk. Use a plastic bag or plastic wrap to tightly wrap the dough. Chill in refrigerator for 1 hour, or until firm.

4. Dust a surface with flour and roll out the dough with a thickness of 1/4 inch. Use cookie cutters to cut preferred cookie shapes and transfer to ungreased cookie sheets. Decorate the cookies with sprinkles or colored sugar. Bake for 13 to 15 minutes and be careful not to brown the cookies. Transfer the cookies to a flat surface right away with a spatula to cool.

Nutrition Information

Calories: 166 calories; Total Carbohydrate: 21.8g Cholesterol: 31 mg Total Fat: 8.1g Proteinr: 1.9g Sodium: 91 mg

SUGAR COOKIES

Serving: 35 - **Prep:** 1h - **Ready in:** 9h10m

INGREDIENTS

- 2 cups white sugar
- 1 cup butter
- 2 tsps. vanilla extract
- 2 eggs
- 6 cups all-purpose flour
- 2 tsps. baking powder
- 2 tsps. baking soda
- 1 cup buttermilk

DIRECTION

1. Beat together vanilla, butter and sugar in a mixing bowl until light colored. Whip in eggs.
2. Sift baking powder and flour together into a large bowl. Dissolve baking soda in buttermilk in a separate small bowl. Mix buttermilk and egg mixture incrementally into the dry mixture. It will form a stiff dough. Put into the refrigerator for overnight.
3. Turn on the oven to 350°F (175°C) to preheat.
4. On a lightly floured surface, roll out dough so that it is 1/4-inch thick. Use cookie cutters to cut and transfer onto cookie sheets.
5. Put into the prepped 350°F (175°C) oven to bake for 8-10 minutes.

Nutrition Information

Calories: 177 calories; Total Carbohydrate: 28.2g Cholesterol: 26 mg Total Fat: 5.8g Proteinr: 2.9g Sodium: 141 mg

SNICKERDOODLES

Serving: 48 - **Prep:** 20m - **Ready in:** 1h

INGREDIENTS

- 1/2 cup butter, softened
- 1/2 cup shortening
- 1 1/2 cups white sugar
- 2 eggs
- 2 tsps. vanilla extract
- 2 3/4 cups all-purpose flour
- 2 tsps. cream of tartar
- 1 tsp. baking soda
- 1/4 tsp. salt
- 2 tbsps. white sugar
- 2 tsps.ground cinnamon

DIRECTION

1. Set the oven to 400°F (200°C), and start preheating.
2. Cream vanilla, eggs, 1 1/2 cups of sugar, shortening and butter together. Blend in salt, soda, cream of tartar and flour. Shape dough into balls with rounded spoonfuls.
3. Mix cinnamon with 2 tbsps. of sugar. Roll dough balls in mixture. Place on ungreased baking sheets and they are 2 inches apart .
4. Bake until set but not too hard, about 8 - 10 minutes. Immediately take away from baking sheets.

Nutrition Information

Calories: 92 calories; Total Carbohydrate: 12.4g Cholesterol: 13 mg Total Fat: 4.3g Proteinr: 1g Sodium: 55 mg

DROP SUGAR COOKIES

Serving: 66 - **Prep:** 20m - **Ready in:** 30m

INGREDIENTS

- 2 1/2 cups all-purpose flour

- 3/4 tsp. salt
- 1/2 tsp. baking soda
- 1 1/2 cups white sugar
- 1/2 cup butter, softened
- 1/2 cup shortening
- 1 tsp. vanilla extract
- 1 egg
- 2 tbsps. milk
- 1 tbsp. white sugar, or as desired

DIRECTION

1. Turn oven to 400°F (200°C) to preheat.
2. Sift together baking soda, salt, and flour into a mixing bowl. In another bowl, beat shortening, butter, vanilla extract, and 1 1/2 cups sugar until well combined. Beat in egg until creamy. Whisk creamed mixture into flour mixture until no lumps remain; whisk in milk. Drop batter onto a baking sheet by tsps.; press each piece using the bottom of a waterglass. Scatter top of each cookie with enough sugar to cover.
3. Bake cookies in the heated oven for 10 to 12 minutes or until their edges turn brown lightly.

Nutrition Information

Calories: 63 calories; Total Carbohydrate: 8.4g Cholesterol: 7 mg Total Fat: 3.1g Proteinr: 0.6g Sodium: 47 mg

MY VERSION OF THE FAMOUS LOFTHOUSE COOKIE

Serving: 12 - **Prep:** 15m - **Ready in:** 47m

INGREDIENTS

- 1 (18.25 oz.) package French vanilla cake mix (such as Duncan Hines Moist Deluxe)
- 3 large eggs
- 1/2 cup all-purpose flour, plus
- 3 tbsps. all-purpose flour
- 1/3 cup soybean oil
- Icing:

- 4 cups confectioners' sugar
- 1/2 cup unsalted butter, at room temperature
- 1/3 cup shortening
- 3 tbsps. half-and-half
- 1 tsp. vanilla extract

DIRECTION

1. Preheat an oven to 165°C/325°F; line silicone baking mats on 2 baking sheets. Beat soybean oil, 3 tbsps. of flour, 1/2 cup of flour, eggs and cake mix till stiff in stand mixer.
2. Divide then roll dough to 1 inch balls; put on prepped baking sheets. Flatten to 1/2-inch thick.
3. In preheated oven, bake for 12 to 14 minutes till somewhat firm in middle; take from oven. Sit cookies till set for 5 more minutes, undisturbed.
4. Spread aluminum foil sheet on countertop; put cookies on foil to fully cool for at least 20 minutes .
5. Use hand mixer to beat vanilla extract, half and half, shortening, butter and confectioners' sugar till smooth; put in pastry bag. Pipe/spread with spatula on cooled cookies.

Nutrition Information

Calories: 552 calories; Total Carbohydrate: 82.1g Cholesterol: 68 mg Total Fat: 24.2g Proteinr: 3.5g Sodium: 298 mg

NUTTY CRISPY SUGAR COOKIES

Serving: 60 - **Prep:** 20m - **Ready in:** 1h10m

INGREDIENTS

- 5 cups all-purpose flour
- 2 tsps. baking soda
- 2 tsps. cream of tartar
- 1/4 tsp. salt
- 1 cup butter
- 2 cups white sugar
- 2 eggs
- 1 cup vegetable oil
- 1 tsp. vanilla extract
- 3/4 cup chopped walnuts

DIRECTION

1. Heat an oven to 175 ° C or 350 ° F. Oil cookie sheets lightly. Mix salt, cream of tartar, baking soda and flour; put aside.
2. Cream sugar and butter in a big bowl till smooth. Whip in vegetable oil, vanilla and eggs. Slowly mix in mixture of flour till smooth. Mix nuts in. Drop rounded teaspoonfuls of dough on prepped cookie sheets. Press using a fork to flatten the cookies.
3. Bake for about 10 to 12 minutes in prepped oven, or till the edges start to turn brown. Let a minute to cool on baking sheets then transfer onto wire racks and fully cool.

Nutrition Information

Calories: 136 calories; Total Carbohydrate: 14.9g Cholesterol: 14 mg Total Fat: 8g Proteinr: 1.5g Sodium: 76 mg

OATMEAL SUGAR COOKIES

Serving: 24

INGREDIENTS

- 1 cup white sugar
- 1 cup shortening
- 2 eggs
- 1 tsp. vanilla extract
- 1 cup rolled oats
- 1/2 cup raisins
- 1 3/4 cups all-purpose flour
- 1 tsp. baking soda
- 1/2 tsp. salt
- 1/2 tsp.ground cinnamon

DIRECTION

1. Cream vanilla, eggs, shortening (you may opt for half a cup of margarine or butter as an alternative) and sugar thoroughly. Stir in the rest of the ingredients. Leave in the fridge for 4-5 hours or overnight.
2. Set oven to 190°C (375°F) and start preheating.
3. Form rounded teaspoonful of dough into balls. Put onto ungreased baking sheet. Usinggreased bottom ofglass dipped in sugar, flatten out each ball. Bake for 10 minutes.

OLD FASHIONED BUTTER COOKIES WITH BUTTER FROSTING

Serving: 72 - **Prep:** 30m - **Ready in:** 3h5m

INGREDIENTS

- 1 cup butter, softened
- 3/4 cup white sugar
- 1 egg
- 2 tbsps. whole milk
- 1 1/2 tsps. vanilla extract
- 3 cups all-purpose flour
- 1 tsp. baking powder
- 1/2 tsp. salt

Frosting:

- 1 cup butter, softened
- 3 cups confectioners' sugar
- 1 1/2 tbsps. vanilla extract
- 9 tbsps. evaporated milk, or more as needed
- 6 cups confectioners' sugar, or more as needed

DIRECTION

1. In a large bowl, beat white sugar with one cup of the softened butter until creamy. Beat one and a half tsps. of vanilla extract, whole milk and egg into the butter mixture until they become smooth. In a separate bowl, whisk salt, baking powder and flour. Stir dry ingredients gradually into the moist ingredients to create the smooth dough. Let chill the dough for 2-3 hours in refrigerator.
2. Start preheating the oven to 400°F (200°C).generously dust flour over a kitchen towel or pastry cloth.
3. On prepared pastry cloth, split the dough into 3 portions and roll each third out to 1/8-in. thick. Using cookie cutters, cut shapes out of rolled dough. Put the cookies onto unoiled baking sheets.
4. Bake cookies in prepared oven for 5-8 mins or until barely browned. Allow the cookies to cool on baking sheets for 5 mins. Then cool completely on a wire rack.

5. In a bowl, beat evaporated milk, 1 1/2 tbsps. of the vanilla extract, 3 cups of the confectioners' sugar and one cup of the softened butter, until they become smooth. Stir 6 cups of confectioners' sugar gradually into the mixture until combined. Beat the frosting hard until it is fluffy. If needed to reach preferred consistency, stir in more confectioners' sugar or evaporated milk. Frost the cooled cookies.

Nutrition Information

Calories: 136 calories; Total Carbohydrate: 21.3g Cholesterol: 17 mg Total Fat: 5.4g Proteinr: 0.8g Sodium: 63 mg

OLD FASHIONED SUGAR COOKIES IN A JAR

Serving: 24 - **Prep:** 15m - **Ready in:** 15m

INGREDIENTS

- 3 cups all-purpose flour
- 1 tsp. baking powder
- 1 tsp. baking soda
- 1/8 tsp. salt
- 1 1/2 cups white sugar
- 1 cup butter, softened
- 2 eggs
- 1 tsp. vanilla extract
- 1/2 tsp. lemon extract

DIRECTION

1. Combine salt, baking soda, baking powder and flour in a medium bowl. Set aside. Add sugar in a layer onto the bottom of a 1 quart large mouth jar and add flour mixture on top. Attach the tag with the following instructions:
2. In a large bowl, pour in the contents of the jar. Add 1 cup of softened butter; cut until crumbly. Whisk 1/2 tsp. of lemon extract, 1 tsp. of vanilla and 2 eggs in a separate bowl until it reaches fluffy and light texture. Combine with the dry ingredients; stir to blend properly. Cover and let it chill for 1 hour.
3. Turn on the oven to 350°F (175°C) to preheat. Roll the dough on a lightly floured surface so that it becomes 1/4 inch thick. Use cookie cutters to cut into preferred shapes. Arrange cookies on cookie sheets, 1 1/2 inches apart from each other.

4. Put into the oven to bake until the edges starts to turn brown, 10-12 minutes. Use sugar for decorations before baking of frost after baking.

Nutrition Information

Calories: 180 calories; Total Carbohydrate: 24.5g Cholesterol: 36 mg Total Fat: 8.2g Proteinr: 2.2g Sodium: 140 mg

OLD TIME SOFT SUGAR COOKIES

Serving: 24 **- Prep:** 10m **- Ready in:** 30m

INGREDIENTS

- 1/2 cup shortening
- 1 cup white sugar
- 1 egg
- 3/4 cup buttermilk
- 1 tsp. vanilla extract
- 2 cups all-purpose flour
- 1/2 tsp. baking soda
- 1/2 tsp. salt

DIRECTION

1. Beat shortening and sugar together. Whisk in vanilla, buttermilk, and egg.
2. Mix salt, baking soda, and flour together; whisk into creamed mixture until incorporated. Refrigerate dough for 1 hour in the fridge. Drop mixture onto a lightly oiled baking sheet by rounded tsps., leaving about 2 inches of space between each cookie. Scatter tops of cookies with white sugar just before serving, if desired.
3. Turn oven to 400°F (205°C) to preheat.
4. Bake cookies in the preheated oven until firm, for 7 to 9 minutes.

Nutrition Information

Calories: 114 calories; Total Carbohydrate: 16.7g Cholesterol: 8 mg Total Fat: 4.6g Proteinr: 1.6g Sodium: 86 mg

OLD-FASHIONED SOFT SUGAR COOKIES

Serving: 18

INGREDIENTS

- 1/2 cup butter
- 1 1/2 cups white sugar
- 2 eggs
- 1 tsp. vanilla extract
- 3 cups sifted all-purpose flour
- 1 tsp. salt
- 1/2 tsp. baking powder
- 1/2 tsp. baking soda
- 1 cup sour crea m
- 6 tbsps. cinnamon sugar

DIRECTION

1. Set the oven to 190°C or 375°F to preheat.
2. Cream butter until achieve mayonnaise's consistency. gradually put in sugar while keeping on creaming.
3. Put in 1 egg at a time while beating well between additions. Put in vanilla and beat until fluffy and light.
4. Mix and sift baking soda, baking powder, salt and flour together in a separate bowl.
5. Put in dry ingredients together with sour cream, alternately, starting and finishing with dry ingredients.
6. Drop by tbsps. or tsps., depending on your preferred size of cookie. Sprinkle over tops of cookies with cinnamon-sugar mixture then bake for about 8-10 minutes.

Nutrition Information

Calories: 238 calories; Total Carbohydrate: 37.3g Cholesterol: 40 mg Total Fat: 8.5g Proteinr: 3.3g Sodium: 229 mg

PARTY SUGAR COOKIES

Serving: 72 **- Prep:** 15m **- Ready in:** 2h

INGREDIENTS

- 1 (3 oz.) package fruit flavored Jell-O mix

- 1 cup white sugar
- 1 cup shortening
- 3 eggs
- 1 tsp. vanilla extract
- 1/2 tsp. salt
- 3 1/4 cups all-purpose flour
- 1 egg white
- 1/4 cup colored sugar for decoration

DIRECTION

1. Heat an oven to 175 ° C or 350 ° F.
2. Cream sugar, shortening and flavoredgelatin in a big bowl till smooth. Whip in eggs, one by one, then mix vanilla in. Mix salt and flour, mix into creamed mixture.
3. Split dough to 4 portions, and chill any dough that is not being used yet. Unroll a dough piece at one time on a slightly floured counter into thickness of quarter-inch. Use cookie cutters to cut dough and arrange on an unprepped cookie sheet. Brush egg white on cookies tops, and scatter colored sugar over.
4. Bake in the prepped oven, about 8 to 10 minutes. Prevent from browning. Cool cookies on cookie sheets for several minutes then remove to wire rack and fully cool.

Nutrition Information

Calories: 67 calories; Total Carbohydrate: 8.9g Cholesterol: 9 mg Total Fat: 3.1g Proteinr: 1g Sodium: 23 mg

PATTERN COOKIES

Serving: 12

INGREDIENTS

- 2/3 cup shortening
- 1 cup white sugar
- 2 eggs
- 1 tsp. vanilla extract
- 1/3 cup milk
- 3 cups all-purpose flour
- 1 tbsp. baking powder
- 1/2 tsp. salt

DIRECTION

1. Cream the sugar and shortening together in a medium-size bowl. Whip in eggs, one by one, then mix in milk and vanilla. Mix baking powder, salt and flour, and mix to wet mixture. Refrigerate with cover, approximately an hour.

2. Heat the oven to 175 ° C or 350 ° F. Line parchment paper on baking sheets. Unroll dough on a slightly floured counter into thickness of 1/4 to 1/8 inch. Use cookie cutters to cut to preferred forms.

3. Bake in prepped oven, about 8 - 10 minutes, till the center of cookie bounces back once tapped. Allow to cool on the wire racks. Ice with icing if wished.

Nutrition Information

Calories: 296 calories; Total Carbohydrate: 41.3g Cholesterol: 32 mg Total Fat: 12.6g Proteinr: 4.5g Sodium: 234 mg

PEPPERMINT BARK SNOWFLAKE COOKIES

Serving: 24 **- Prep:** 25m **- Ready in:** 1h20m

INGREDIENTS

- 1 roll Pillsbury refrigerated sugar cookie dough
- 3 tbsps. all-purpose flour
- 1 cup white vanilla baking chips
- 1 tbsp. vegetable oil
- 1/3 cup blue candy melts
- 1/3 cup creme de menthe baking chips

DIRECTION

1. Heat an oven to 375°F. Break cookie dough up in big bowl; work in flour thoroughly. Use 1/2 dough at a time, refrigerate leftover dough till needed.

2. Roll dough to 1/4-in. thick on work surface lightly sprinkled with flour; use 2 1/2-3-in. snowflake-shaped floured cookie cutters to cut. Put on ungreased cookie sheets, 1-in. apart. Repeat with leftover dough; reroll scraps.

3. Bake till edges just start to brown and cookies are set or for 7-10 minutes; cool for a minute. Transfer from cookie sheets onto cooling racks. Cool completely for about 10 minutes.

4. Meanwhile, microwave vegetable oil and white vanilla baking chips in medium microwaveable bowl, uncovered, for 1-2 minutes, mixing every 30 seconds, on 50% Medium till smooth. Spread mixture over cookies; put on cooking parchment paper/waxed paper sheet close together. Set for 5 minutes.

5. Microwave crème de menthe chips and blue candy melts in different medium microwavable bowls, each for 1-2 minutes, uncovered, on 50% medium, mixing every 30 seconds, till smooth. Drizzle with crème de menthe chips and candy melts, using 2 small spoons on white chips.

Nutrition Information

Calories: 177 calories; Total Carbohydrate: 22.1g Cholesterol: 7 mg Total Fat: 8.9g Proteinr: 1.8g Sodium: 77 mg

PEPPERMINT HOT COCOA COOKIES

Serving: 20 - **Prep:** 30m - **Ready in:** 1h

INGREDIENTS

- 1 roll Pillsbury refrigerated sugar cookie dough
- 3 tbsps. unsweetened baking cocoa
- 1 cup marshmallow creme
- 1/3 cup crushed peppermint candies

DIRECTION

1. Preheat the oven to 350 ° F. Tear cookie dough apart in medium size bowl. Work baking cocoa in to combine well.

2. Form dough into 20 balls of 1 1/2-inch. Put onto unoiled cookie sheets, and use your fingers to flatten down a bit. Bake till middles of cookies are firm, about 10 to 13 minutes; cool on pans for 2 minutes. Remove onto cooling racks for 15 minutes to fully cool.

3. Meantime, remove marshmallow creme to microwave-safe cup coated in cooking spray using spatula coated in cooking spray. Microwave with no cover to melt for 1 minute to 1 1/2 minute on Medium or 50%. Cool partially, then put to sealable food-storage plastic bag.

4. Snip off 1/8-inch from a bag corner, then sprinkle marshmallow creme on cookies, and scatter crushed peppermint candies over. Chill for not less than half an hour yet no more than 12 hours prior to serving.

Nutrition Information

Calories: 139 calories; Total Carbohydrate: 22.9g Cholesterol: 8 mg Total Fat: 5g Proteinr: 1g Sodium: 70 mg

PERFECT VEGAN SUGAR COOKIES

Serving: 30 - **Prep:** 15m - **Ready in:** 55m

INGREDIENTS

- 2 cups all-purpose flour
- 1 tsp. baking soda
- 1/4 tsp. salt
- 3/4 cup white sugar
- 1/2 cup vegan margarine (such as Earth Balance)
- 1 tsp. vanilla extract
- 2 tbsps. coconut milk

DIRECTION

1. Set an oven to preheat to 175°C (350°F). Line parchment paper on 2 baking trays.
2. Sift the salt, baking soda and flour into a bowl.
3. In a bowl, cream the vegan margarine and sugar using an electric mixer for about 2 minutes, then add the vanilla extract. Mix in the flour mixture, then add the coconut milk, 1 tbsp. at a time, until the dough comes together. Wrap it using plastic wrap and let it chill for 30 minutes.
4. On a floured surface, roll out the dough to 1/4 to 1/2-inch thick. Dip the cookie cutter in the flour, then cut out the cookies and put it on the prepped baking trays.
5. Let it bake in the preheated oven for about 10 minutes, until it turns light golden in color.

Nutrition Information

Calories: 71 calories; Total Carbohydrate: 11.4g Cholesterol: 0 mg Total Fat: 2.5g Proteinr: 0.9g Sodium: 86 mg

PERFECT VEGAN SUGAR COOKIES AND ICING

Serving: 36 - **Prep:** 15m - **Ready in:** 10h27m

INGREDIENTS

- 1 cup margarine

- 1 cup white sugar
- 1 tbsp. egg substitute (such as Ener-G Egg Replacer)
- 1 tsp. vanilla extract
- 3 3/4 cups all-purpose flour
- 1/4 cup tofu cream cheese (such as Tofutti)
- 2 tsps. baking powder
- 2 cups confectioners' sugar
- 2 tbsps. vanilla soy milk (such as Silk), or more to taste
- 3 drops assorted food coloring, or as desired
- 1/2 tsp. almond extract
- 4 tsps. light corn syrup

DIRECTION

1. In a large bowl, beat together sugar and margarine with an electric mixer until they are creamy. Mix in vanilla extract and egg substitute. Slowly put in baking powder, flour, and cream cheese. If necessary, stir into dough with your hands. Shape the dough into long loaf. Cover with cellophane. Place in the refrigerator at least 120 mins or until firm.
2. Start preheating oven to 350°F (175°C). Line baking sheets with aluminum foil or lightly coat.
3. On lightly floured surface, roll the dough out into 1/4-in. thickness. Using cookie cutters, cut into preferred forms. Arrange on baking sheets about 1 in. apart.
4. Bake in prepared oven for 12-14 mins or until edges and bottoms just begin to turn light brown. Discard the cookies from the baking sheets. Put on wire racks to cool. Preserve in airtight container.
5. In a bowl, stir together soy milk and confectioners' sugar until they become smooth. Beat in almond extract and corn syrup until the icing isglossy and smooth. If it's too thick, putting in more corn syrup. Put in the food coloring to preferred intensity. Submerge cookies into icing; allow to dry about 8 hours or up to overnight.

Nutrition Information

Calories: 146 calories; Total Carbohydrate: 23g Cholesterol: < 1 mg Total Fat: 5.4g Proteinr: 1.5g Sodium: 94 mg

PHILIPPINE-MADE SUGAR COOKIE

Serving: 50 - **Prep:** 20m - **Ready in:** 35m

INGREDIENTS

- 2 1/2 cups all-purpose flour
- 1 tsp. baking soda
- 1/2 tsp. baking powder
- 1/4 tsp. salt
- 1 cup butter, softened
- 1 cup white sugar
- 2 eggs
- 1 tsp. vanilla extract
- 8 oz. semisweet chocolate,grated

DIRECTION

1. Heat an oven to 175 ° C or 350 ° F. Oil or line cookie sheets with aluminum foil or parchment paper. Sift salt, baking powder, baking soda and flour together; put aside.
2. Cream sugar and butter in a big bowl till fluffy and light. Whip in eggs, one by one then mix vanilla in. Mixture must be pale yellow and thick. Slowly mix in sifted ingredients till incorporated thoroughly. Drop teaspoonfuls of dough, on prepped cookie sheets, spacing 3- inches away. Scatter cookies tops withgrated chocolate.
3. Bake in prepped oven for 12 to 15 minutes, till cookies start to brown surrounding the edges. Transfer from cookie sheets onto wire racks and let cool. Keep in cookie jar, airtight.

Nutrition Information

Calories: 96 calories; Total Carbohydrate: 11.4g Cholesterol: 17 mg Total Fat: 5.4g Proteinr: 1.3g Sodium: 69 mg

PINK ICING COOKIES

Serving: 24 - **Prep:** 15m - **Ready in:** 25m

INGREDIENTS

- 1 cup butter
- 2 cups white sugar
- 4 eggs
- 1 cup milk
- 5 cups all-purpose flour
- 1/2 tsp. salt

- 3 tsps. baking powder
- 1 tsp. vanilla extract

DIRECTION

1. Turn oven to 350°F (175°C) to preheat. Butter a cookie sheet.
2. Cream together margarine and butter in a large mixing bowl. Beat in eggs, one at a time, until combined. Whisk in vanilla and milk. Stir together baking powder, salt, and flour; mix into creamed mixture until well incorporated. Drop cookie dough onto thegreased cookie sheet by heaping spoonfuls.
3. Bake cookies in the preheated oven until tops spring back when touched lightly like a cake, approximately 10 to 12 minutes. Allow to cool on wire racks before adding frosting.

Nutrition Information

Calories: 245 calories; Total Carbohydrate: 37.3g Cholesterol: 52 mg Total Fat: 9g Proteinr: 4.2g Sodium: 180 mg

POINSETTIA COOKIES

Serving: 48 - **Prep:** 45m - **Ready in:** 1h25m

INGREDIENTS

- 3/4 cup butter, softened
- 2/3 cup white sugar
- 1 (3 oz.) package cream cheese, softened
- 1 tsp. vanilla extract
- 1 egg
- 2 cups all-purpose flour
- 1 tsp. red food coloring
- 1 cup red decorator sugar
- 1 cup confectioners' sugar, sifted
- 2 tsps. water
- 1 drop yellow food coloring

DIRECTION

1. Heat an oven to 175 ° C or 350 ° F. Line parchment paper or aluminum foil on baking sheets.
2. Cream the sugar, cream cheese and butter using an electric mixer in a big bowl till fluffy and light. Put in vanilla and egg; combine to blend thoroughly. While putting sufficient red food coloring, mix in flour

using your hand with sturdy spoon, turning dough into a pretty red color.

3. Roll the balls in red decorator sugar and arrange them on prepped cookie sheets an- inch away. Chill the cookies for approximately 10 minutes on cookie sheets till set.

4. Create 3 cuts along every cookie once they are firm, creating 6 slices resembling a pie, do not cut all the way through the cookie balls just till approximately 2/3 of the way.

5. Bake about 10 to 12 minutes in prepped oven, till cookies look dry. Let cool on cookie sheets, then remove from aluminum foil.

6. Combine water and confectioners' sugar to reach a piping consistency to create frosting for cookies. Put in one yellow food coloring drop. Place the frosting in sealable bag or pastry bag and snip off a small piece from corner. Pipe tiny dots on the middle of cookies. Dry frosting before keeping cookies at room temperature in airtight container. Keep cookies for maximum of 2 weeks.

Nutrition Information

Calories: 89 calories; Total Carbohydrate: 13.6g Cholesterol: 13 mg Total Fat: 3.7g Proteinr: 0.8g Sodium: 27 mg

POLVARONES

Serving: 36 **- Prep:** 15m **- Ready in:** 31m

INGREDIENTS

- 1/2 cup white sugar
- 1/2 cup butter
- 1/2 cup shortening
- 1 tbsp. almond extract
- 2 1/2 cups all-purpose flour
- 2 tbsps. colored sugar, or as desired (optional)
- 2 tbsps. sprinkles, or as desired (optional)
- 2 tbsps.guava paste, or as desired (optional)

DIRECTION

1. Preheat oven to 175°C or 350°F.
2. Use an electric mixer to beat shortening, butter and white sugar together in a bowl till creamy. Stir in almond extract. In batches, add flour and knead the dough till combined thoroughly.
3. Roll dough into balls with the size of a walnut; place on baking sheet, 2 in. apart. Use a wooden spoon handle to make a well in each cookie. Drizzle guava paste, sprinkles and colored sugar into the wells.

4. Bake for 16-20 minutes in the preheated oven till lightly golden in color.

Nutrition Information

Calories: 100 calories; Total Carbohydrate: 11.3g Cholesterol: 7 mg Total Fat: 5.6g Proteinr: 0.9g Sodium: 18 mg

POWDERED SUGAR COOKIES I

Serving: 48

INGREDIENTS

- 1 cup confectioners' sugar
- 1 cup white sugar
- 1 cup butter
- 1 cup vegetable oil
- 1 pinch salt
- 2 eggs
- 1 tsp. baking soda
- 1 tsp. cream of tartar
- 1 tsp. vanilla extract
- 4 cups all-purpose flour

DIRECTION

1. Beat salt, vegetable oil, margarine and sugars thoroughly. Put in dry ingredients and eggs .
2. Shape into balls, roll in sugar then arrange 1 inch apart on ungreased cookie sheet.
3. Bake at 350°F (175°C) for 8 minutes. Roll in colored sugar instead of white sugar if you want something more special for holidays.

Nutrition Information

Calories: 142 calories; Total Carbohydrate: 14.7g Cholesterol: 18 mg Total Fat: 8.7g Proteinr: 1.4g Sodium: 60 mg

POWDERED SUGAR COOKIES II

Serving: 40

INGREDIENTS

- 1/2 cup shortening
- 1/2 cup butter
- 1 1/2 cups confectioners' sugar
- 1 egg
- 1 tsp. vanilla extract
- 1/4 tsp. almond extract
- 2 1/2 cups sifted all-purpose flour
- 1 tsp. baking soda
- 1 tsp. cream of tartar
- 1 cup chopped pecans

DIRECTION

1. Beat butter and shortening. Slowly mix in powdered sugar (confectioners' sugar) until well creamed. Add flavorings and eggs. Beat until fluffy.
2. Sift together cream of tartar, baking soda, and flour; put and mix well into the batter. Mix in pecans.
3. Drop batter on unoiled baking sheets by small teaspoonfuls (or small balls). Bake for 8 to 10 minutes at 400°F (205°C) until cookies have creamy tan color. Roll cookies in powdered (confectioners') sugar while they are hot.

Nutrition Information

Calories: 110 calories; Total Carbohydrate: 10.9g Cholesterol: 11 mg Total Fat: 7g Proteinr: 1.2g Sodium: 50 mg

POWDERED SUGAR COOKIES III

Serving: 36

INGREDIENTS

- 1 cup butter flavored shortening
- 1 egg
- 1 cup confectioners' sugar
- 1 tsp. vanilla extract
- 1 tsp. cream of tartar
- 1/2 tsp. salt

- 1 tsp. baking soda
- 2 cups all-purpose flour

DIRECTION

1. Combine egg, confectioners' sugar and shortening. Mix in flour, baking soda, salt, cream of tartar and vanilla. Combine thoroughly.
2. Form the dough into balls, an-inch in diameter. Arrange onto cookie sheet. Flatten using a sugared bottom ofglass. Or you may also use sugared cookie stamps.
3. Bake approximately 10 minutes at 175 ° C or 350 ° F or barely till edges are becominggolden. Cool partially then remove from cookie sheet.

Nutrition Information

Calories: 93 calories; Total Carbohydrate: 8.7 g Cholesterol: 5 mg Total Fat: 6.2g Proteinr: 0.9g Sodium: 69 mg

PRETZEL-TOPPED SUGAR COOKIES

Serving: about 4-1/2 dozen. - **Prep:** 15m - **Ready in:** 30m

INGREDIENTS

- 2 tubes (18 oz. each) refrigerated sugar cookie dough
- 2-1/2 cups vanilla or white chips, divided
- 1 package (7-1/2 oz.) white fudge-covered pretzels

DIRECTION

1. Crush cookie dough into small pieces into a large mixing bowl; add 1 1/2 cups chips and mix well, drop mixture onto ungreased baking sheets by tablespoonfuls, separating mounds 2 inches apart.
2. Bake cookies for 15 to 18 minutes at 325° until lightly browned. Instantly insert a pretzel into the center of each cookie. Transfer cookies to wire rack and allow to cool.
3. Melt the rest of chips in a microwave oven; whisk until no lumps remain. Drizzle over cookies togarnish.

Nutrition Information

Calories: 102 calories Total Carbohydrate: 13g Cholesterol: 5 mg Total Fat: 5g Fiber: 0g Proteinr: 1g Sodium: 60 mg

PRIZE-WINNING SUGAR COOKIES

Serving: 24

INGREDIENTS

- 1 cup butter
- 2 cups white sugar
- 3 eggs
- 1 cup buttermilk
- 1 tsp. baking soda
- 1 pinch salt
- 4 1/2 cups sifted all-purpose flour
- 4 tsps. baking powder
- 1/4 cup vanilla extract
- 1 tsp.ground nutmeg

DIRECTION

1. Set oven to 350° F (180° C) to preheat.
2. Cream the sugar and margarine well. Put in the eggs, 1 at a time, beating thoroughly after each addition. Put in the buttermilk.
3. Sift the baking powder, salt, baking soda and flour together and put into the creamed mixture.
4. Put in nutmeg and 1/4 cup of vanilla (yes, this is correct), and thoroughly blend. Allow dough to rest for 10 minutes.
5. Ongreased cookie sheet, drop by tablespoonfuls. Sprinkle additional sugar on top.
6. Bake for 10 minutes.

Nutrition Information

Calories: 238 calories; Total Carbohydrate: 35.6g Cholesterol: 44 mg Total Fat: 8.7g Proteinr: 3.6g Sodium: 208 mg

PUMPKIN SPICE SOFT SUGAR COOKIES

Serving: 48 - **Prep:** 15m - **Ready in:** 20m

INGREDIENTS

- 1 1/2 cups butter, softened
- 2 cups white sugar
- 2 eggs
- 2 tsps. vanilla extract
- 3 1/2 cups all-purpose flour
- 1 tbsp. pumpkin pie spice
- 1 tsp. baking powder
- 1 tsp. salt
- cooking spray
- 1/4 cup white sugar, or as needed

DIRECTION

1. In a large bowl, beat 2 cups of sugar and butter with an electric mixer until it is creamy. Put in vanilla and eggs; then beat until they become smooth.
2. In a bowl, sift together salt, baking powder, pumpkin pie spice and flour. Put the flour mixture into the butter mixture; beat until the flour is incorporated completely. Cover the dough in the plastic wrap. Place in the refrigerator at least 60 mins, until chilled.
3. Start preheating the oven to 375°F (190°C). Spray cooking spray over the baking sheets.
4. Pour a quarter cup of sugar into a shallow bowl.
5. Drop dough by spoonfuls placing 2-inch apart onto the prepared baking sheets. Moistenglass bottom with water; dipglass in the sugar. Using bottom of sugaredglass, flatten each drop of cookie doughgently.
6. Bake cookies in prepared oven for 5-7 mins, until set.

Nutrition Information

Calories: 124 calories; Total Carbohydrate: 16.5g Cholesterol: 23 mg Total Fat: 6.1g Proteinr: 1.3g Sodium: 103 mg

QUESO FRESCO SUGAR COOKIES

Serving: 36 - **Prep:** 20m - **Ready in:** 31m

INGREDIENTS

- 2 1/2 cups all-purpose flour
- 1 tsp. baking soda

- 1/2 tsp. baking powder
- 1/2 tsp. salt
- 1 1/2 cups white sugar
- 3/4 cup butter, at room temperature
- 3/4 cup queso fresco, at room temperature
- 1 egg
- 1 tbsp. vanilla extract

DIRECTION

1. Line two baking sheets with parchment paper and set an oven to 350 degrees F or 175 degrees C.
2. In a big bowl, combine together salt, baking powder, baking soda, and flour.
3. In big bowl, beat together queso fresco, butter, and sugar, then add in the egg, mixing well to combine. Beat in vanilla extract then mix the flour mixture in slowly, pouring in 1 cup at a time, until the dough combines completely.
4. Shape each tablespoonful of dough into even balls and place them on the baking sheets 1 inch apart.
5. Bake in the oven for 9 - 11 minutes until they are set and cool on baking sheets for 2 minutes. Move them onto wire racks to completely cool.

Nutrition Information

Calories: 108 calories; Total Carbohydrate: 15.3g Cholesterol: 17 mg Total Fat: 4.5g Proteinr: 1.7g Sodium: 110 mg

RUM SUGAR COOKIES

Serving: 48 - **Prep:** 20m - **Ready in:** 2h30m

INGREDIENTS

- 3 cups all-purpose flour
- 1/2 tsp. baking soda
- 1/2 tsp. salt
- 1/2 tsp. baking powder
- 1 cup butter
- 2 eggs
- 1 cup white sugar
- 1 tsp. rum flavored extract
- 1/2 tsp. almond extract

- 1/8 tsp. ground nutmeg

DIRECTION

1. Combine butter, baking powder, salt, baking soda and flour until the mixture looks like cornmeal.
2. Mix nutmeg, almond extract, rum extract, sugar and eggs together until well combined. Add the egg mixture into the flour mixture. Stir until well mixed. Separate the dough into two equally. Keep the dough in the fridge for 2 hours.
3. Preheat the oven to 350°F (175°C).
4. On a lightly floured surface, add dough. Roll out the dough to 1/8 inch thickness. Cut the dough into cookies with a cookie cutter (in any shapes you want). Arrange the cookies on an ungreased baking sheet.
5. Bake in the preheated oven for 7-9 minutes, till the edges are golden. Cool the cookies on the baking sheet in 1 minute, then add onto a wire rack for cooling completely.

Nutrition Information

Calories: 82 calories; Total Carbohydrate: 10.2g Cholesterol: 18 mg Total Fat: 4.1g Proteinr: 1.1g Sodium: 73 mg

RUMFORD SUGAR COOKIES

Serving: 24

INGREDIENTS

- 2 cups white sugar
- 1 cup shortening
- 3 eggs
- 2 tbsps. water
- 3 tsps. baking powder
- 1 tsp. ground nutmeg
- 1/2 tsp. ground cloves
- 3 cups all-purpose flour

DIRECTION

1. Cream together sugar and fat; whip in whipped eggs. Put in 1 cup of flour and baking powder, then put in spices and water. Put in the remaining flour gradually; adding more flour until the dough is stiff enough to roll. On pastry board, sprinkle flour. Form the dough into a ball; transfer it onto the board.

Use flour to rub on rolling pin and roll out so that it is 1/4-inch thick. Cut in round cakes; usegranulated sugar to sift over each and put into the oven to bake quickly at 400 to 450 degrees F (200-230 degrees C).

Nutrition Information

Calories: 207 calories; Total Carbohydrate: 28.9g Cholesterol: 23 mg Total Fat: 9.4g Proteinr: 2.4g Sodium: 70 mg

SUPER SUGAR COOKIE S

Serving: 24 - **Prep:** 15m - **Ready in:** 55m

INGREDIENTS

- 5 1/2 cups all-purpose flour
- 1 tsp. cream of tartar
- 1 tsp. baking soda
- 1/4 tsp. salt
- 2 cups butter, room temperature
- 2 cups white sugar
- 1 tsp. vanilla extract
- 2 large eggs

DIRECTION

1. Turn oven to 350°F (175°C) to preheat. Line parchment paper onto a baking sheet.
2. Sift together salt, baking soda, cream of tartar, and flour in a large bowl.
3. Beat together white sugar and butter in a large mixing bowl using an electric mixer until fluffy and light. Add vanilla extract and beat well. Put in eggs, one by one, mixing well between additions. Slowly add flour; beat on low speed just until incorporated.
4. Cut dough into 4 pieces; chill 3 pieces of dough in the fridge. Flatten the remaining dough out to 1/4-inch thick on a work surface lightly dusted with flour. Cut out desired shapes using cookie cutters; remove to the prepared baking sheet.
5. Bake cookies in the preheated oven until edges turngolden slightly, for 10 to 12 minutes. Let cookies cool for 5 minutes on the baking sheet; transfer to a wire rack and let cool completely. Repeat the steps of rolling, cutting as well as baking with the rest of dough.

Nutrition Information

Calories: 311 calories; Total Carbohydrate: 38.7g Cholesterol: 56 mg Total Fat: 16g Proteinr: 3.6g Sodium: 192 mg

SANTA HAT COOKIES

Serving: 48 - **Prep:** 30m - **Ready in:** 1h10m

INGREDIENTS

- 1 (16 oz.) package Pillsbury Ready to Bake!™ sugar cookies
- 1 (7 oz.) jar marshmallow creme
- 1 cup butter, softened
- 2 1/2 cups powdered sugar
- 1/2 tsp. redgel food color
- 48 miniature marshmallows
- White candy sprinkles

DIRECTION

1. Preheat the oven to 350 ° F. Halve every cookie. Form every half into ball. Arrange on unoiled cookie sheets an-inch away.
2. Bake till edges turngolden brown and are set, about 10 to 12 minutes. Cool on cookie sheets for 5 minutes then remove onto cooling rack. Cool fully for 10 minutes.
3. To prep icing, whip softened butter and marshmallow creme in a big bowl on moderate speed of an electric mixer to blend. Whip powdered sugar in till fluffy. Put in food color, and whip to combine thoroughly.
4. Put the icing in sealable food-storage plastic bag. Snip off a small corner of bag. Pipe icing on every cookie top, mounding in shape of a hat.
5. Put mini-marshmallow over every hat. Press sprinklesgently surrounding bottom edge of every hat to ensure they adhere to icing.

Nutrition Information

Calories: 120 calories; Total Carbohydrate: 16.5g Cholesterol: 10 mg Total Fat: 5.9 g Proteinr: 0.3g Sodium: 55 mg

SCARLETT'S BEST EVER SUGAR COOKIES

Serving: 100 - **Prep:** 16m - **Ready in:** 45m

INGREDIENTS

- 1 cup confectioners' sugar
- 1 cup packed brown sugar
- 1 cup butter
- 1 cup vegetable oil
- 2 egg
- 2 tsps. vanilla extract
- 4 1/4 cups all-purpose flour
- 1 tsp. baking soda
- 1 tsp. salt
- 1 tsp. cream of tartar
- 1 cup chopped pecans
- 1/3 cupgranulated sugar for decoration

DIRECTION

1. Turn oven to 350°F (175°C) to preheat.
2. Whisk together butter, oil, and sugar in a large bowl. Whisk in vanilla and eggs. Mix cream of tartar, salt, baking soda, and flour together. Add to the creamed mixture and stir to combine. Fold in pecans. Shape dough into walnut-sized balls. Arrange balls onto unbuttered sheet. Flatten each ball using the bottom of aglass coated with sugar. (You can use aglass with decorative bottom to have beautiful-patterned cookies).
3. Bake cookies in the preheated oven for 10 minutes or until edges turngolden brown.

Nutrition Information

Calories: 80 calories; Total Carbohydrate: 8.3g Cholesterol: 9 mg Total Fat: 5g Proteinr: 0.8g Sodium: 51 mg

HEART SUGAR COOKIES

Serving: 15 - **Prep:** 20m - **Ready in:** 32m

INGREDIENTS

- 2/3 cup butter, softened
- 1 cupgranulated sugar, or more to taste
- 2 eggs, beaten
- 1 tsp. baking soda
- 1 tsp. vanilla extract
- 1 1/4 tsps. cream of tartar
- 1/4 cup milk
- 4 cups all-purpose flour
- 1 pinch salt (optional)
- 1 cup all-purpose flour

DIRECTION

1. Turn oven to 400°F (200°C) to preheat.
2. In a large bowl, beat sugar and butter using an electric mixer until fluffy. Put in 1 egg, mixing well until incorporated with butter mixture before putting in the next with vanilla extract.
3. Whisk cream of tartar into milk until dissolved; mix into the butter mixture; add a pinch of salt and 4 cups flour; beat until a dough forms.
4. Coat a flat work surface with 1 cup flour. Roll dough out on the floured surface; cut out desired shapes until all dough is used up.
5. Bake cookies for approximately 12 minutes on nonstick baking sheets at 400°F (200°C) until cookies are firm in the center.

Nutrition Information

Calories: 288 calories; Total Carbohydrate: 45.6g Cholesterol: 44 mg Total Fat: 9.3g Proteinr: 5.3g Sodium: 153 mg

SNICKERDOODLES

Serving: 36 - **Prep:** 15m - **Ready in:** 30m

INGREDIENTS

- 1 cup shortening
- 1 1/2 cups white sugar
- 2 eggs

- 2 3/4 cups all-purpose flour
- 1 tsp. baking soda
- 2 tsps. cream of tartar
- 1/2 tsp. salt
- 2 tbsps. white sugar
- 2 tsps.ground cinnamon

DIRECTION

1. Preheat an oven to 190°C/375°F.
2. Cream 1 1/2 cups sugar and shortening in a medium bowl; mix in eggs. Sift salt, cream of tartar, baking soda and flour together; mix into creamed mixture till blended well. Mix cinnamon and 2 tbsp. sugar in a small bowl. Roll dough to walnut-size balls; roll balls in cinnamon-sugar. Put onto unprepped cookie sheet, 2-in. apart .
3. In the preheated oven, bake till edges are slightly browned for 8-10 minutes; transfer to wire racks. Cool.

Nutrition Information

Calories: 125 calories; Total Carbohydrate: 16.5g Cholesterol: 10 mg Total Fat: 6.1g Proteinr: 1.3g Sodium: 71 mg

SNOWFLAKE SUGAR COOKIES

Serving: 24 - **Prep:** 30m - **Ready in:** 1h38m

INGREDIENTS

- 3 cups flour
- 1/2 tsp. baking powder
- 1/4 tsp. salt
- 1 cup butter, softened
- 1 cup sugar
- 1 egg
- 2 tsps. lemon extract (optional)
- Colored sprinkles
- 2 cups powdered sugar
- Milk
- Reynolds Parchment Paper

DIRECTION

1. Turn on the oven to 375°F to preheat. Use Reynolds(R) Parchment Paper to line cookie sheet; set aside.
2. Use an electric mixer to beat together sugar and butter to fluffy. Add lemon extract and egg; beat to well-combined.
3. In a separate bowl, mix together salt, baking powder and flour. Add flour mixture to butter mixture and slowly beat so that it is smooth. Cut the dough into 2 pieces; press into 2 flat disks to shape. Use parchment paper to wrap dough; put into the refrigerator for 1 hour until it is firm enough to roll.
4. Place the dough between 2 sheets of parchment paper that have been lightly floured and roll until it is 1/8-inch thick.
5. Use 2-to-6-inch snowflake cookie cutters to cut the dough. Transfer cookies to cookie sheet lined with parchment paper, 1-inch away from each other. Use colored sprinkles to decorate. Put into the oven to bake until the edges of the cookies begin to brown or for 8-10 minutes. Let them cool.
6. In a small bowl, combine milk and powdered sugar; pour milk in slowly to adjust the consistency to your liking. Pour slightly onto the cooled cookies.

Nutrition Information

Calories: 205 calories; Total Carbohydrate: 31.2g Cholesterol: 28 mg Total Fat: 8.2g Proteinr: 2g Sodium: 93 mg

SOFT BIRTHDAY CAKE COOKIES

Serving: 48 - **Prep:** 20m - **Ready in:** 55m

INGREDIENTS

- 1 cup white sugar
- 1/2 cup butter, softened
- 1/2 cupgreek yogurt
- 2 eggs
- 1 tsp. vanilla extract
- 1 1/2 cups all-purpose flour
- 1 1/2 cups white whole wheat flour
- 1 1/2 tsps. baking powder
- 1/2 tsp. baking soda
- 2/3 cup sprinkles

Frosting:

- 1/2 cup butter, softened
- 3 cups confectioners' suga r
- 1 tsp. vanilla extract
- 1 tsp. heavy cream, or as needed (optional)
- 1/2 cup sprinkles (optional)

DIRECTION

1. Turn on the oven to 350°F (175°C) to preheat. Use parchment paper to line 2 baking sheets. In a bowl of a stand mixer, mix together butter and sugar; beat until fluffy and light. Whip in vanilla extract, eggs andgreek yogurt. Put in baking soda, baking powder, whole wheat flour and all-purpose flour; stir until mixed. Add sprinkles and fold.
2. With a cookie scoop, scoop out even amounts of dough; form to balls. On the prepped baking sheets, place balls. Flatten the balls with aglass or hand.
3. Put into the prepped oven to bake for 10 to 12 minutes until edges are lightlygolden. Remove to a cooking rack; continue with the rest of dough. Let the cookies cool fully for about 15 minutes. While cookies are cooling, make the frosting. Whisk butter until creamy; combine with the confectioners' sugar. Mix in vanilla extract. If necessary, use cream to thin the frosting. With a knife, add frosting to cookies and spread out. Use more sprinkles to cover.

Nutrition Information

Calories: 137 calories; Total Carbohydrate: 21.3g Cholesterol: 19 mg Total Fat: 5.4g Proteinr: 1.4g Sodium: 61 mg

SOFT CHRISTMAS COOKIES

Serving: 48 - **Prep:** 20m - **Ready in:** 3h

INGREDIENTS

- 3 3/4 cups all-purpose flour
- 1 tsp. baking powder
- 1/2 tsp. salt
- 1 cup margarine, softened
- 1 1/2 cups white sugar
- 2 eggs
- 2 tsps. vanilla extract

DIRECTION

1. Sift together salt, baking powder, and flour; put aside. Cream together the sugar and margarine in a big bowl until fluffy and light. Whisk in eggs, 1 egg each time, and then mix in vanilla. Slowly mix in the sifted ingredients until completely incorporated. Put a cover on the dough and refrigerate for 2 hours.
2. Turn the oven to 400°F (200°C) to preheat. Coat the baking sheets with oil. On a surface scattered with flour, roll a bit of the chilled dough until having 1/4-in. thickness. Use cookie cutters to cut out shapes.
3. Bake in the preheated oven for 6-8 minutes until just turning brown around the edges. Transfer from cookie sheets to wire racks to cool.

Nutrition Information

Calories: 97 calories; Total Carbohydrate: 13.8g Cholesterol: 8 mg Total Fat: 4g Proteinr: 1.3g Sodium: 81 mg

SOFT FROSTED SUGAR COOKIES

Serving: 36 **- Prep:** 20m **- Ready in:** 1h

INGREDIENTS

- 1 cup vegetable shortening
- 1 cup white sugar
- 1/4 cup milk
- 2 eggs
- 1 tsp. vanilla extract
- 3 cups all-purpose flour
- 1 tsp. salt
- 1 tsp. baking soda
- 1/4 cup butter
- 3 cups confectioners' sugar
- 1 1/2 tsps. vanilla extract, or more to taste
- 2 tbsps. milk, or as needed

DIRECTION

1. Set oven to preheat at 350°F (175°C).
2. Beat together 1 tsp. vanilla extract, white sugar, 1/4 cup milk, eggs, and vegetable shortening in a bowl. Whisk together baking soda, salt, and flour in a different bowl. Beat the mixture of flour into the mixture

of shortening slowly till a smooth dough forms.

3. Roll dough out on a floured work surface to the thickness of 1/4 inch and cut into shapes. Place the cookies onto baking sheets.
4. In the preheated oven, bake till cookies are firm, about 10 minutes. Let them cool down.
5. Use an electric mixer to beat together 2 tbsps. milk, confectioners' sugar, 1 1/2 tsps. vanilla extract, and butter in a bowl on high speed until frosting is slightly fluffy and spreadable. Frost onto the cooled cookies.

Nutrition Information

Calories: 166 calories; Total Carbohydrate: 23.6g Cholesterol: 14 mg Total Fat: 7.4g Proteinr: 1.5g Sodium: 114 mg

SOFT SUGAR COOKIES II

Serving: 36

INGREDIENTS

- 1 cup butter, softened
- 2 1/4 cups white sugar
- 2 eggs
- 5 cups all-purpose flour
- 1 tsp. baking soda
- 1/2 tsp. baking powder
- 1 1/2 tsps.ground cardamom
- 1/2 cup milk

DIRECTION

1. Cream 2 cups of sugar and butter together in a big mixing bowl. Put in 1 egg at a time and beat well between additions. Mix together 1 tsp. of cardamom, baking powder, baking soda and flour, then put into the creamed butter mixture together with milk, alternately.
2. Mix cardamom and leftover sugar together in a separate small bowl then dip into sugar/cardamom mixture with rounded teaspoonfuls of dough.
3. Place coated dough ongreased baking sheets and bake at 190°C or 375°F until browned slightly, about 10 to 12 minutes. Allow to cool on wire racks.

Nutrition Information

Calories: 163 calories; Total Carbohydrate: 26g Cholesterol: 24 mg Total Fat: 5.6g Proteinr: 2.3g Sodium: 84 mg

SOFT SUGAR COOKIES III

Serving: 30

INGREDIENTS

- 1 cup packed brown sugar
- 1 cup white sugar
- 1 cup butter
- 1 cup sour cream
- 3 eggs
- 1 tsp. baking powder
- 1 tsp. baking soda
- 3 cups all-purpose flour

DIRECTION

1. Set the oven to 220°C or 425°F to preheat and coat cookie sheets lightly withgrease.
2. Cream together sugar and butter until fluffy and light, then put in eggs and blend thoroughly.
3. Put into the butter mixture with baking soda, baking powder and flour together with sour cream, alternately.
4. Drop on prepared cookie sheets with teaspoonfuls of dough and bake at 220°C or 425°F for about 8 minutes.

Nutrition Information
Calories: 177 calories; Total Carbohydrate: 23.8g Cholesterol: 38 mg Total Fat: 8.4g Proteinr: 2.2g Sodium: 115 mg

SOFT SUGAR COOKIES IV

Serving: 24

INGREDIENTS

- 2/3 cup shortening

- 2/3 cup butter
- 1 1/2 cups white sugar
- 2 eggs
- 2 tsps. vanilla extract
- 3 1/2 cups all-purpose flour
- 2 tsps. baking powder
- 1 tsp. salt
- 1/3 cupgranulated sugar for decoration

DIRECTION

1. Set oven to 350°F (175°C) to preheat.
2. Beat sugar, shortening, and butter in a medium mixing bowl. Whisk in vanilla and eggs. Mix salt, baking powder, and flour together; mix into creamed mixture until incorporated. Shape dough into walnut-sized balls, then roll in sugar. Arrange cookies about 2 inches apart on an ungreased cookie sheet.
3. Bake cookies in the preheated oven for 10 to 12 minutes or until bottom turns brown lightly. Transfer cookies from the baking sheets to wire racks to cool.

Nutrition Information

Calories: 228 calories; Total Carbohydrate: 29.4g Cholesterol: 29 mg Total Fat: 11.4g Proteinr: 2.5g Sodium: 180 mg

SOFT SUGAR COOKIES

Serving: 48 - **Prep:** 20m - **Ready in:** 30m

INGREDIENTS

- 4 cups all-purpose flour
- 1 tsp. baking powder
- 1/2 tsp. baking soda
- 1/2 tsp. salt
- 1/4 tsp.ground nutmeg
- 1 cup butter, softened
- 1 1/2 cups white sugar
- 1 egg
- 1 tsp. vanilla extract

* 1/2 cup sour cream

DIRECTION

1. Sift nutmeg, flour, baking powder, baking soda, and salt together; put to one side. Whisk together butter and sugar in a large bowl until no lumps remain. Beat in sour cream, vanilla, and egg until incorporated. Mix in the sifted ingredients. Wrap dough in plastic wrap; refrigerate overnight.
2. Turn your oven to 375°F (190°C) to preheat. Flatten dough to a thickness of 1/4 inch on a work surface lightly dusted with flour. Cut out desired shapes with cookie cutters. Lay cookies on ungreased cookie sheets, placing them 1 1/2 inches apart.
3. Bake cookies in the preheated oven for 8 to 10 minutes. Let cookies cool for 5 minutes on the baking sheet; transfer to a wire rack to cool entirely.

Nutrition Information

Calories: 103 calories; Total Carbohydrate: 14.3g Cholesterol: 15 mg Total Fat: 4.5g Proteinr: 1.3g Sodium: 75 mg

SOFT SUGAR COOKIES WITH WHITE CHOCOLATE, ALMONDS, AND CRANBERRIES

Serving: 78 - **Prep:** 15m - **Ready in:** 35m

INGREDIENTS

* 1 cup shortening
* 1 cup butter, softened
* 2 1/4 cups white sugar
* 3 eggs
* 1 tbsp. vanilla extract
* 1 tsp. almond extract
* 5 1/4 cups all-purpose flour
* 1 tbsp. baking powder
* 1 1/2 tsps. salt
* 1 cup slivered almonds, chopped
* 1 cup white chocolate chips
* 1 (6 oz.) package cherry-flavored sweetened dried cranberries (such as cherry-flavor Craisins)

DIRECTION

1. Preheat an oven to 175°C/350°F.
2. Use electric mixer to beat butter, shortening and sugar till smooth in big bowl; beat almond extract, vanilla extract and eggs into butter mixture.
3. Whisk salt, baking powder and flour in bowl; add flour mixture to butter mixture slowly just till dough comes together. Mix dried cranberries, white chocolate chips and almonds into dough.
4. Drop rounded dough tbsps. on baking sheets, 2-in. apart. Bake cookies for 10-12 minutes till bottom edges become lightgolden brown. Cool for 5 minutes. Transfer to wire rack; completely cool.

Nutrition Information

Calories: 129 calories; Total Carbohydrate: 15.5g Cholesterol: 14 mg Total Fat: 6.8g Proteinr: 1.6g Sodium: 80 mg